I0430236

TM 10-420

WAR DEPARTMENT

TECHNICAL MANUAL

EMERGENCY FOOD PLANTS AND POISONOUS PLANTS

OF THE

ISLANDS OF THE PACIFIC

April 15, 1943

TM 10-420

TECHNICAL MANUAL

❦

EMERGENCY FOOD PLANTS AND POISONOUS PLANTS

OF THE

ISLANDS OF THE PACIFIC

UNITED STATES
GOVERNMENT PRINTING OFFICE
WASHINGTON : 1943

For sale by the Superintendent of Documents, U. S. Government Printing Office
Washington, D. C.

TM 10-420

Emergency Food Plants

and Poisonous Plants of

the Islands of the Pacific

This Edition Copyright © 2013 by SOA Books

Layout, graphics, design and cover by: SOA Books

All rights reserved. No part of this book may be reproduced in any form by any electronic or mechanical means including photocopying, recording, or information storage and retrieval without permission in writing from the author.

ISBN-13: 978-1484113523
ISBN-10: 1484113527

Printed in U.S.A

WAR DEPARTMENT
WASHINGTON, April 15, 1943.

TM 10–420, Emergency Food Plants of the Islands of the Pacific, was written by Dr. E. D. Merrill, Administrator of Botanical Collections and Director of the Arnold Arboretum, Harvard University, and is published for the information and guidance of all concerned.

[A. G. 062.12 (2–22–43).]

BY ORDER OF THE SECRETARY OF WAR:

G. C. MARSHALL,
Chief of Staff.

OFFICIAL:
    J. A. ULIO,
        Major General,
            The Adjutant General.

DISTRIBUTION:
    IC (24).
    (For explanation of symbols see FM 21–6.)

TABLE OF CONTENTS

LIST OF ILLUSTRATIONS

LIST OF ILLUSTRATIONS

LIST OF ILLUSTRATIONS

TECHNICAL MANUAL

EMERGENCY FOOD PLANTS AND POISONOUS PLANTS OF THE ISLANDS OF THE PACIFIC

SECTION I

PURPOSE AND SCOPE

	Paragraph
Purpose	1
Scope	2

■ 1. PURPOSE.—The purpose of this manual is to aid the individual who becomes separated from his unit by illustrating and describing the edible and poisonous plants so that this individual can live off the land. The natives of the Malayan and Polynesian regions use parts of a great many wild plants as food, sometimes to supplement and diversify their daily diet, and sometimes as famine foods in time of scarcity. The parts used include young shoots and leaves of various herbs, shrubs, and trees, various fruits, certain seeds, some flowers and flower buds, and the tubers or starchy bulblike roots of various cultivated and wild plants. Some of these plant parts have a high food value and some are rich in vitamins.

■ 2. SCOPE.—*a. Region covered.*—This manual covers all of Polynesia, Micronesia, and Melanesia, as well as the entire Malay Archipelago including the Malay Peninsula and the Philippines. For all practical purposes it also covers Indo-China, Thailand (Siam), Burma, and eastern India.

b. Plants.—The more common plants that occur in reasonable abundance that may be used as food in times of emergency are included. The following have been excluded:

(1) Rare species.

(2) Plants that are familiar to residents of the temperate regions including maize or Indian corn, sorghum, rice, pineapple, cabbage, carrot, beet, garden bean, squash, cucumber, egg plant, sweet pepper, and other universally cultivated food plants.

(3) Familiar fruit trees such as the orange, lime, pomelo (one of the parents of the grapefruit), lemon, etc.

SECTION II

REASSURANCE AND WARNING

■ 3. JUNGLE SNAKES.—There is altogether too much fear of the Tropics, particularly on the part of those individuals without previous tropical experience. Thus the widespread fear of "the snake infested jungle" is an entirely imaginary picture. Poisonous snakes are absent from Polynesia. In Malaysia, they are very rare and are seldom seen. *The chances of being bitten by a poisonous snake in any part of the Malayan region are very much smaller than in any part of the United States where rattle snakes and water moccasins occur.*

■ 4. POISONOUS PLANTS.—*a. General.*—There is no reason to fear the small number of poisonous plants in any part of Polynesia or Malaysia. The general rule is to avoid the following:

(1) Those with milky sap (except the numerous species of wild fig).

(2) All plants the taste of which is disagreeable.

b. Contact poisons.—In the Malayan and Polynesian region there are few contact poisons corresponding to our poison ivy, poison sumac, and poison oak. However, they all belong to the same natural family of plants (*Anacardiaceae*). The poisonous principle is the same and the treatment is the same as that indicated for persons coming in contact with poison ivy. In the Malay Peninsula, Sumatra, Java, and Borneo where most of them occur, they are collectively known as *rengas* and are all small to large trees. A few of the wild or semiwild species of mango, but not the common mango, also have poisonous sap. These are sometimes cultivated or sometimes found in the forests. In the Malay Peninsula, Sumatra, Java, and Borneo, rarely outside of this region, they are known as *kemang, lanjut, binjai, bachang, kwini* and *wani*. Normally an individual might be poisoned

2

by these species when engaged in actually felling the trees. Their poisonous properties are thoroughly well known to the natives. Curiously, the fruits of all of these wild and semi-wild types of mango can be safely eaten, even when the sap is poisonous.

c. *Stinging plants.*—There are some types of plants, never very common, that have stinging hairs such as the tree nettles (*Laportea*) (par. 24d) and the cowhage (*Mucuna*) (par. 24e). These stinging hairs of the latter are merely mechanical irritants and are not poisonous.

■ 5. JUNGLE PESTS.—Keep constantly in mind the fact that in all of Malaysia and Polynesia there is almost no danger from poisonous snakes, noxious insects, spiders, and poisonous plants. The forests and jungles of the entire region are a distinctly safe place in which to operate under anything even approaching normal conditions. The malaria mosquito and the land leech are the pests to avoid whenever possible. The land leech is found only in the high forests during the rainy season, or in the areas where the rainfall is heavy in all months of the year.

SECTION III

ASSISTANCE AND ADVICE OF NATIVES

■ 6. NATIVE USE OF PLANTS.—In all parts of the region the natives in general know both the wild and the cultivated plants which may be used as food. However, in certain sections, for example, Java, their use as food may be known but quite unknown to the natives of other islands in Malaya, Micronesia, and Polynesia. The breadfruit, which is a basic food in many parts of Polynesia, is little used as food in most parts of Malaya, where the species also occurs, simply because better foods are usually available there. A great many plants used by the natives of Java as food are quite unknown as food plants elsewhere.

⊠ 7. ADVICE OF NATIVES.—Whenever possible, try to get in touch with natives even though one may be able to talk with them only by means of signs. They can be most helpful in times when regular rations are not available. They usually know how these emergency food plants should be prepared, and those which may be poisonous if eaten raw. In some of the actually poisonous plants the poisonous principle may be eliminated by proper cooking, or by other treatments, and the material then eaten with entire safety.

⊠ 8. LOCAL NAMES.—In selecting recorded native plant names, no attempt has been made to indicate in what islands and by what peoples the names are used. In the area covered, there are probably in excess of 450 or 500 different languages or dialects involved. For all plants of this vast region there are probably in excess of 50,000 native plant names actually recorded; many locally used plant names are still unlisted. Some native plant names are very widely used, while others are local. Many of the plants considered have no common names in English.

SECTION IV

MISCELLANEOUS INFORMATION

⊠ 9. PLANTS NEAR THE SEASHORE.—The number and variety of plants on the atolls and low islands of Polynesia and Micronesia are usually small, whether the islands be small or large, inhabited or uninhabited. Naturally, a greater variety of food plants, many of them cultivated, are found on the inhabited islands. On most islands will be found on or near the seashore such plants as the pandan or screw pine (par. 22*y*), common purslane (par. 20*j*), seaside purslane (par. 20*k*), *Boerhaavia* (par. 20*l*), Polynesian arrowroot (par. 19*j*), and such shrubs and trees as *Ximenia* (par. 22*ab*), *Morinda* (par. 20*ad*), *Tournefortia* (par. 20*ac*), *Pemphis* (par. 20*ab*), *Thespesia* (par. 20*aa*), and *Erythrina* (par. 20*y*), as well as various weedy herbs, such as *Alternanthera* (par. 20*g*),

4

Emilia (par. 20*r*), *Amaranthus* (par. 20*e*), *Commelinaceae* (par. 20*c*), and perhaps some other introduced weeds considered in this manual. Even on uninhabited islands is sometimes found the coconut palm (par. 16*e*), and the breadfruit (par. 22*c*), where casual visitors have planted them. Generally, the vegetation on these low islands is very simple, with very few species as compared with that of the high islands, such as Fiji, Samoa, and others, and with the individual islands of the Malayan region.

■ 10. GUIDE FOR EATING FRUITS.—Keep in mind that those cultivated trees and shrubs growing in the settled areas, in and near towns, that bear attractive fleshy fruits, for the most part are actually planted for their fruits, and that generally their fruits may be eaten with perfect safety. In the wild, where monkeys occur, a safeguard to follow is to observe what the monkeys actually eat in the form of wild fruits. The feeding habits of birds is not such a safe guide. One should keep in mind constantly that fruit maturity in the tropics is normally seasonal just as it is in temperate regions, and only occasionally, as with the coconut palm, are fruits produced throughout the year.

SECTION V

EDIBLE FERNS

■ 11. FERNS IN GENERAL.—The number of different kinds of ferns in the Malayan-Polynesian region is very great, probably exceeding 1,500 different species. Some are small insignificant, while others are relatively very large in size, including the characteristic tree ferns (par. 12). Parts of certain species of ferns are regularly used as food by the natives and these parts are often offered for sale in native markets. While the food value of the edible parts of ferns is probably relatively low, yet these parts will help sustain life when other foods are not available. In general the parts most commonly used are the young unfolding leaves, commonly spoken of as "fiddle heads;" these may be eaten either raw or cooked. Some of these "fiddle heads" are too tough, and others are bitter or otherwise bad tasting. But one point may be kept in mind that, so far as known, none of the ferns is actually poisonous when eaten. In some species the young

FIGURE 1.—Tree ferns (*Cyathea*).

tender leaves are cooked and eaten. In general only a few of the better known or useful ferns have definite plant names, but a common collective name for all ferns in the Malay Archipelago is *pako* or *paku*.

6

■ 12. SPECIFIC FERNS.—*a. Tree ferns (Cyathea)*.—Being chiefly forest ferns, tree ferns may sometimes be found in deserted clearings especially in more or less constantly wet

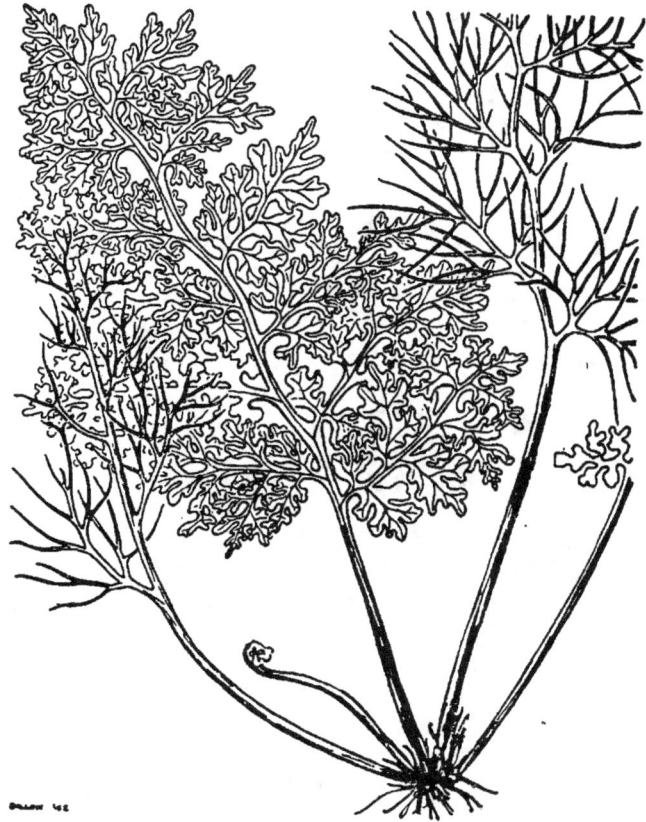

FIGURE 2.—Swamp fern (*Ceratopteris thalictroides*).

regions. There are many different kinds and they are often abundant and are sometimes up to 25 feet high or even more. The young leaves as they commence to uncurl, the so-called "fiddle heads," are tender and may be eaten raw

7

or cooked. The terminal tender bud or "cabbage" may also be eaten. Local names: *Éki, ákii, biúng, óli-óli, paóga, pákuitam, pákis-ádji, gíro*.

b. *Swamp fern (Ceratopteris thalictroides)*.—This fern, often occurring in great abundance, is found in very wet soil, old rice paddies, and swampy places, more or less submerged. It never occurs in salt or brackish swamps. The whole plant which is 1 to 1½ feet high may be cooked and eaten as greens, or may be eaten uncooked. It is an excellent food. Local names: *Pákis-rawa, sájor-kódok*.

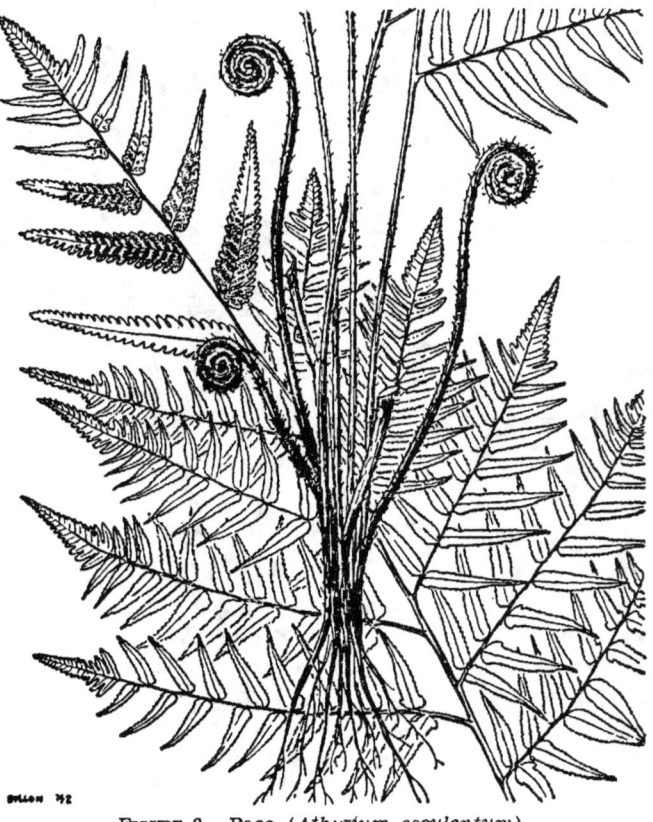

FIGURE 3.—Paco (*Athyrium esculentum*).

8

c. Paco (Athyrium esculentum).—This fern often occurs in great abundance along swift-running streams, margins of rivers, and in some fresh-water swamps. It is usually about 2 feet high. The young developing leaf stalks, or

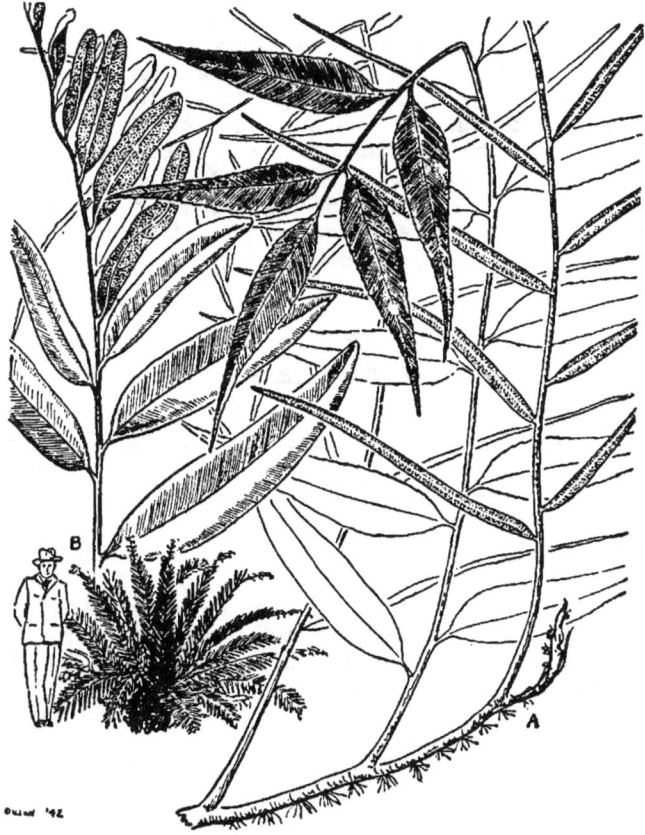

FIGURE 4.—A, *Stenochlaena palustris;* B, *Acrostichum aureum.*

"fiddle heads," are an excellent food and may be eaten in quantity either raw or cooked. Local names: *Páko, páku, Páku-sájor, páku-tándjung, laminding, úta-háu, úta-páso, úta-wáu úta-wásu, pákis-wílis.*

9

d. Stenochlaena palustris and *Acrostichum aureum.*—The tender young leaves of both these ferns may be cooked and eaten. The *Stenochlaena* (A) (fig. 4) is a climbing fern, occurring often in abundance near the inner margins of mangrove swamps, within the influence of salt or brackish water; other species occur in the inland forests. The *Acrostichum* (B) is a very coarse tufted fern, varying from 2 to 6 feet high, its mature leaves being very leathery. It grows only in brackish swamps and hence always near the seashore where it is commonly abundant. Local names. (A, *Stenochlaena*), *Diliman, giliman, lamidin, lemiding, agnáya, hagnáya, ákar-pákis, mélat, miding, páku-ramiding, páku-limbeh, páku-merah, páku-údang, pákis-voráng, wéwésu, bémpésu.* (B, *Acrostichum*). *Lágolo, lángayo, háppasén, sáato, lau-taputá, páku-laut, paku-tiai, péye, piai, kerakás, kalakúk.*

Section VI

EDIBLE HERBS

■ **13. Araceae in General.**—*a.* These plants belonging in the calla lily family are found in the forests and in the open country, varying in size from small to very large herbs. None of the climbing ones should be used for food. Their vegetative parts are in general characterized by being supplied with myriads of minute needlelike stinging crystals of calcium oxalate that are intensely irritating when brought in contact with mucous membranes of the nose, mouth, and throat and, in some cases, even in contact with tender skin; these microscopic crystals (and they occur in our common Indian turnip or Jack-in-the-pulpit) cause the so-called acrid "taste" of these plants, but in spite of the very intense irritation they may cause, the plants are normally not actually poisonous. In spite of the presence of these stinging crystals a considerable number of these plants are regularly eaten and several are widely cultivated for food, such as the taro (and the yautia in tropical America), and to a

less degree the *Cyrtosperma* and *Alocasia.* In these cultivated forms, the underground part is usually greatly enlarged, forming a tuber very rich in starch; thus to a very
considerable degree these tubers take the place of the common potato in the Tropics where a starchy food is needed
to help maintain a balanced diet. The taro tuber in particular is a very excellent well-flavored vegetable. The taro
leaves may be cooked and eaten, although the fresh leaves
are abundantly supplied with the minute stinging crystals,
which in the uncooked leaves are very irritating.

b. In general, when considering any of the numerous
species of this family as food (other than the tubers of the
taro), *one should keep constantly in mind the usual presence of these microscopic stinging crystals of oxalate of lime
and avoid putting any part of the raw plant into the mouth.*
The application of heat breaks down these stinging crystals
so by thoroughly cooking the plant parts that are abundantly supplied with these very irritating needlelike crystals
they may be safely eaten. However, in most cases, the first
"taste" of the cooked aroid should be on the basis of a very
small quantity, and if irritation results the material should
be cooked for a longer period of time.

■ 14. SPECIFIC ARACEAE.—*a. Taro (Colocasia esculenta).*—
This is one of the most commonly cultivated food plants in
Polynesia, and also in the Malayan region, usually grown in
wet lands. The many varieties are usually 1½ feet high. The
tubers are rich in starch and may be eaten in quantity, either
boiled or roasted. They are an excellent substitute for the
potato. The young leaves are commonly eaten as greens,
*but as they contain very many minute stinging crystals they
must be thoroughly boiled before eating,* as the application
of heat destroys these irritating crystals. Local names: *Táo,
tálo, táro, tále, tálas, táles, táleh, tálos, táleus, kálo, súne,
gábi, keládi, kuládi, étu, lúmbu, súkat, ambárgo, saúhat, géte,
béte, kúdjang, lóle, lóee, lóeh, málau, bólang, gélo, lómak, óle,
kóle, kóre, kórei, wóngkai, aládi, tálok, pátjo, súli, rónan,
gwái, kétu, étu, hákar, wákal, inan, ináno, ináne, géhut, kálen,
mom, warimu, hekére, búge, mengkódo, kemb, kom, kómo,
diládo.*

FIGURE 5.—Taro (*Colocasia esculenta*).

b. Schizmatoglottis calyptrata.—This low smooth herb grows as high as 2 or 3 feet, and its flowers are usually yellowish-green, or the upper part is white. It occurs in moist shady places, especially in rocky soils, in forests, sometimes in thickets, and often near streams. All parts of the plant may be cooked and eaten. Local names: *Njampon, wewéhan, solempat, salimpar, sájor-bábi, kesési, tunak, apau, gógu-awa, bábu-banga, apalayi.*

12

c. Elephant ear (Alocasia macrorrhiza).—A very large plant growing in the forests and in open places, the elephant ear sometimes lacks a well-defined trunk, sometimes with a

FIGURE 6.—*Schizmatoglottis calyptrata.*

fairly tall trunk, and is often common and sometimes cultivated. It varies in height from 3 feet to as much as 12 feet. *The juice is very acrid,* due to the presence of thousands of

13

tiny needlelike crystals of oxalate of lime. In contact with the nose and mouth they cause the most intense pain. In times of emergency the softer parts of the trunk, which contains considerable starch, may be cooked and eaten. Some varieties are much more irritating than others.

FIGURE 7.—Elephant ear (*Alocasia macrorrhiza*).

Warning: Do not eat unless first cooked very thoroughly with two or three changes of water. Whenever possible, seek the advice of informed natives who know how to prepare the plant parts as food. Local names: *Taámu, fága, láce, sapúkin, via-míla, via-gága, drámu, píga, ta'ámu, ápe, kápe, papáo-apáka, papáo-atúlong, ába, badiang, biga, abába, bira, bio, sénte, kiáwa, kei, ląwira.*

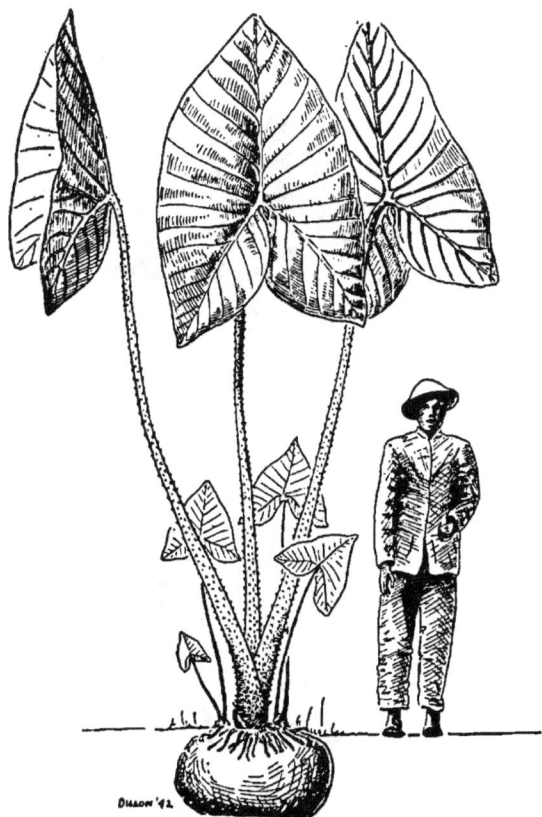

FIGURE 8.—*Cyrtosperma chamissonis.*

d. (*Cyrtosperma chamissonis*).—This is a very large plant *growing only in fresh-water swamps* or swampy places more or less in the open. The leaf stalks are more or less covered with short spines. Sometimes it is cultivated. The large underground part is rich in starch, but is to be eaten *only when thoroughly cooked,* either boiled or roasted. Local names: *Gáliang, pálau, paláuan, bába, búra, puraka, buráka, máota, pulá'a, ápe, ápe-véo, vía-kána, opéves, láck.*

15

e. Amorphophallus campanulatus.—This plant, often common, has large flowers ((A, fig. 9) a foot or more in diameter *appearing before the leaves* (B). The flowers are purplish and mottled and have the odor of decaying meat.

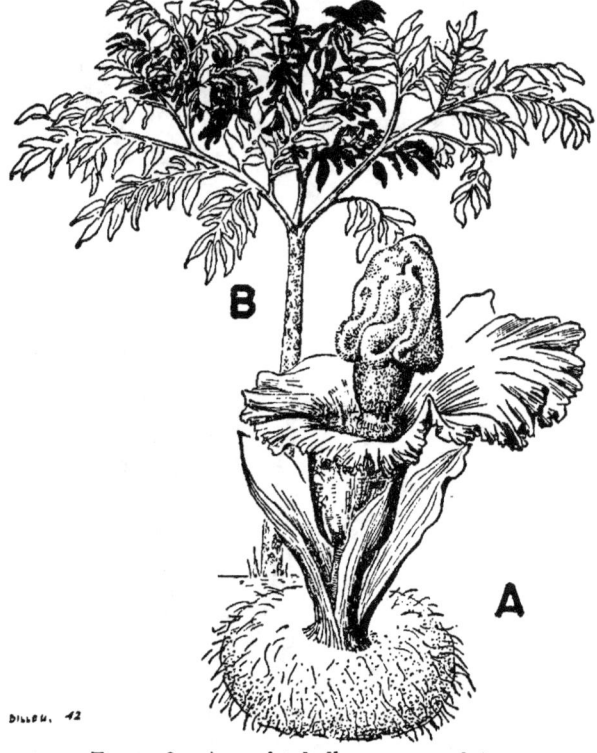

DILLON. 42

FIGURE 9.—*Amorphophallus campanulatus.*

It is found in open places, near thickets, etc., and is sometimes cultivated. The characteristic leafy stem (B) is usually about 3 or 4 feet high. *The tender, young, rather rough and grayish-mottled leaf stems may be eaten, but only after cooking.* The large tuber is rich in starch, but it contains innumerable minute stinging needlelike crystals which

16

are intensely irritating to mucous membranes. *Warning: The large tuber should never be eaten except after prolonged cooking.* Long cooking breaks down the stinging crystals. If possible, consult informed natives before using this as food. Local names: *Púngapung, téve, daíga, dága, málree, súweg, kémbang-bángah, kémbang-bánke, átjung, iléus, bádur, bádul, iles-iles, iléus, wálur, átjung, tjúmpleng.*

SECTION VII

EDIBLE PALMS

■ **15. PALMS IN GENERAL.**—*a.* There are a great many different palms in Malaysia and in Polynesia. They vary greatly in size and in habit. Some are very tall climbers, such as the rattan palms, others low and almost shrubby, and still others are gigantic in size. Some species grow along the seashore within the influence of the salt water, such as the nipa palm, some in open country, others in the secondary forests and thickets, and still others in the high forest.

b. Representatives of several genera (*Corypha, Arenga, Caryota, Metroxylon*) store up great quantities of starch in their trunks (par. 16). This starch is entirely used up by the plant when it produces flowers and fruits, after which the plant dies. This starch is a valuable food, that from *Metroxylon* (par. 16*a*) being the commercial sago. The starch from all of these palms is used for food. The palms are felled, split, the softer inner parts of the trunk crushed, and the starch washed out into troughs to settle. The water is then drawn off and the wet mass which dries is almost pure starch. The usual way of utilizing this starch for food is to make it into cakes which are then baked or roasted. The trunks of *Caryota, Metroxylon,* and *Arenga* are not large and can be manipulated rather easily; that of *Corypha* is gigantic, up to 3 feet in diameter, and the outside is very hard. In attempting to extract starch from any of these it is always best to enlist the services of natives. In any case select the trunks of palms that have not flowered, or, better, those that are just commencing to produce flowers.

17

c. In times of real emergency portions of the starch-bearing softer inner parts of these palm trunks may be cut into pieces which are then roasted or even boiled, after which the starch can be "chewed out" of the fibrous mass that forms the inner parts of the trunk. Its food value is high.

d. In general the terminal bud or "cabbage" of most palms is edible and may be eaten raw, boiled, or roasted. This palm "cabbage," except in those cases where it may be too bitter, is an excellent vegetable. *This bud or "cabbage" is the actual growing tip of the trunk and is found deep in the terminal crown of leaf stalk bases.*

e. In the climbing rattan palms (par. 16c), which are particularly abundant in the high forests and of which there are many different species, the terminal bud or "cabbage" is edible; in many species the lower foot or so of the small trunk contains considerable amounts of starch. In cases of emergency these lower parts may be cut off, roasted over a fire, and the starch then "chewed out." The abundant small fruits of some of the species may be eaten, but the pulp is acid and scanty.

f. Very excellent, clear, tasteless or nearly tasteless drinking water may be obtained from the very long stems of the rattan palms. Cut the stems into about 6- to 8-foot lengths and hold these upright; the water will flow in a small stream from the lower end. In a short time the flow will stop and when this happens cut about a foot off the top end, and the flow will commence again. Repeat until all of the water is obtained. The rattan palms are all high climbers, mostly very spiny on the leaf stalks and leaves and with long slender whiplike spiny appendages, the spines forming characteristic sharp claws. The very long slender stems are smooth and of the same diameter throughout. The stems vary from 10 or 15 feet to several hundred feet in length.

g. Except for the coconut palm and a very few others, the fruits of most of the Old World palm species are not edible. In fact, those of *Arenga* and *Caryota* are very dangerous as they are charged with myriads of minute needle-shaped stinging crystals that cause intense pain when in contact with nose or mouth or even the tender skin. *Warning: In testing palm fruits as to edibility, try only a very small quan-*

tity first. If immediate intense pain results, this means the presence of microscopic stinging crystals. Among the palms it is chiefly in the fruits of *Caryota* and *Arenga* that these intensely irritating stinging crystals occur, and one should never attempt to eat the fruits of these particular palms (par. 16*d*).

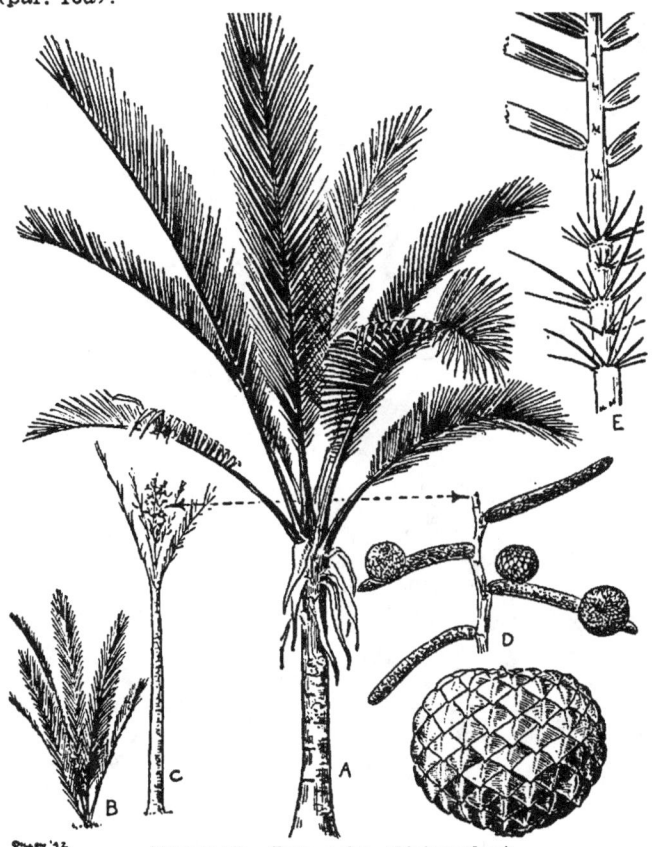

FIGURE 10.—Sago palm (*Metroxylon*).

■ 16. SPECIFIC PALMS.—*a. Sago palm (Metroxylon).*—This palm is found chiefly in fresh-water swamps and is one of the very few palms growing in such places. The tree is

19

usually 25 to 30 feet high and smooth and very spiny forms occur. The trunk contains great quantities of starch which is the commercial sago and which is a basic food for the natives in many parts of Malaya. (A) (fig. 10) is a full-grown palm; (B), a young palm; (C), a palm past maturity in fruit, the starch in the trunk all used up by plant; (D) flower and fruit bearing parts and a mature fruit; (E), lower part of a leaf of the spiny form. For brief dis-

FIGURE 11.—*Salacca edulis.*

20

cussion of method of extraction of the starch, see paragraph 15. The terminal buds or "cabbage" may be cooked and eaten as a vegetable. Local names: *Rumbia, rambia, póhon, ságu, lúmbai, lumbíag, búlung, kersúla, resúla, humbia, bái, báir, lípia, rípia, lápia, náwia, tesárak, béri, no, inómo, húda, ambólong, bágsang.*

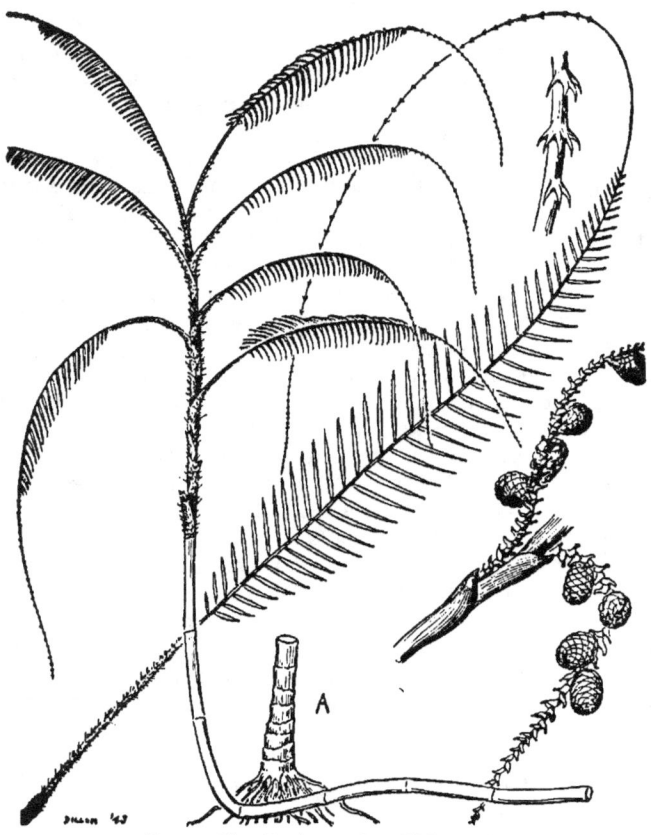

FIGURE 12.—Rattan palm (*Calamus*).

21

b. Salacca edulis.—This is a tufted, spiny, almost stemless palm which grows up to 15 feet high. It bears round, brown fruits which are covered with scales. The yellowish white, sour-sweet, edible pulp surrounding two or three rather large hard seeds may be eaten raw. The immature fruits may also be cooked and eaten. Normally this palm is not found in forests but usually is planted. Local names: *Sálak, búah-sálak, hákam, túsum, seekúmai.*

c. Rattan palm (Calamus).—There are many different kinds of rattan palm and they are found chiefly in the high forest. They are all climbing palms. The leaf stalks and growing parts are very spiny; the stems are smooth and vary in size from the thickness of a pencil to 2 inches in diameter. They are often several hundred feet long. The leaf tips are greatly extended and supplied with numerous very sharp, hard, clawlike teeth. The small growing point or "cabbage" of most species is edible. In many species the lower foot or two of the trunk ((A), fig. 12) is slightly thickened and contains some starch; these lower parts may be roasted and the cooked starch "chewed out." *The stems yield excellent drinking water* (see par. 15).

d. Buri palm; fishtail palm; sugar palm.—All of these palms, like the sago palm, store up great quantities of starch in the softer inner parts of their trunks which may be used as food. (See par. 15.) The tender buds or "cabbage" of all may be cooked and eaten. All of these occur in open lands and in secondary forests; the fishtail palm occurs also in the high forest. The buri palm is recognized by its enormous size, often 50 feet high, its great fan-shaped leaves, and their very stout spiny leaf stalks; the fishtail palm by the shape of its leaves; and the sugar palm by its very long feather-shaped ascending leaves, the lower parts of the leaf stalks where they join the stem with many very long black stiff hairs. Local names: *(Corypha): Búri, gáwang, gébang, silar, silal, tiláda, táli, siger. (Caryota): Anibong, batikan, pugáhan, takipan, gendúru, andúdu, ramisi, áni, pálun, báru, (Arenga): Kaong, kabo-négro, hidiok, idiok, irrok, hánu, áren, ánau, semáki, dalúku.*

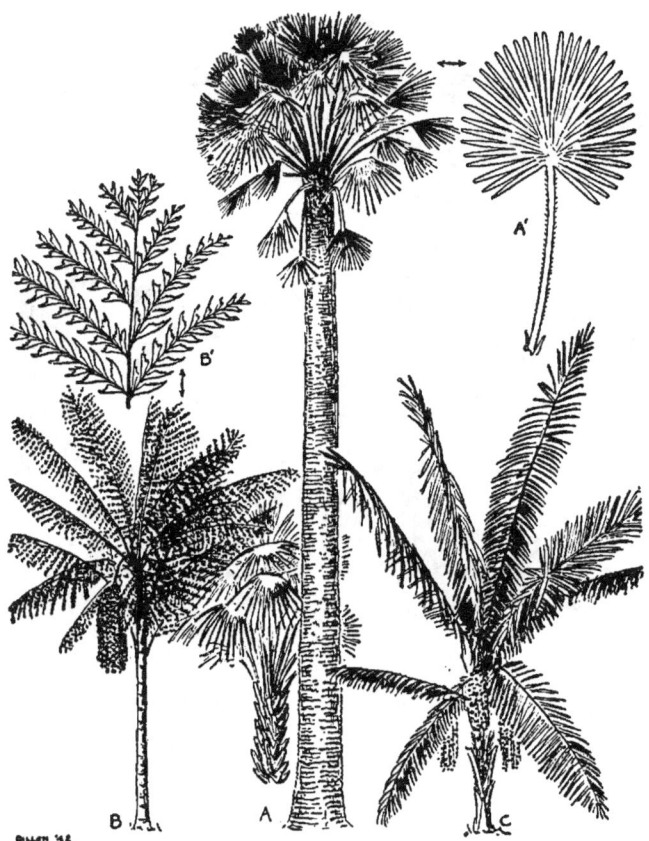

FIGURE 13.—A, Buri palm (*Corypha*, a young palm at the left); B, Fishtail palm (*Caryota*); C, Sugar palm (*Arenga*).

e. Coconut (*Cocos nucifera*).—This plant is one of the most commonly cultivated palms throughout Polynesia and Malaya. The large terminal bud or "cabbage" is one of the very finest vegetables, and may be eaten in quantity, either raw or cooked. The nut yields the very best drinking water that is available anywhere, while the meat may be eaten in

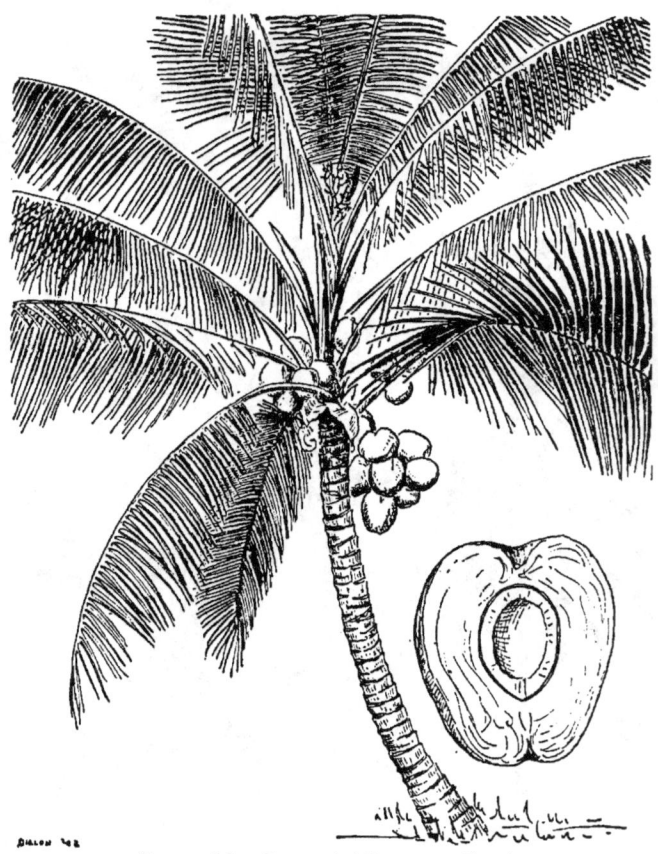

FIGURE 14.—Coconut (*Cocos nucifera*).

any stage of development. Local names: *Nu, ni, niu, nius, nihau, niwéur, niél, igo, nizok, niog, harámbir, arámbir, óḥi, kalápa, njéjong, ṅjur, ṅjir, lángai, óngat, tápo, niúka, bánga, bóngo, kalúku, utíri, turíri, niyog, nóe mérau, éfo, époh, báku, krámbil, krámbir, tuivaloh, kelámbir, váte.*

f. Nipa palm (Nipa fruticans).—This palm occurs only along tidal streams and back of the mangrove swamps where it is always within the influence of salt or brackish water.

FIGURE 15.—Nipa palm (*Nipa fruticans*).

In favorable habitats it sometimes covers hundreds of acres. It is a stemless palm, the part corresponding to the trunk creeping in the mud and sending up several long leaves. The normal height is about 15 feet. The solitary, dark, brown round heads of fruits are about 1 foot or more in diameter. The large white seeds may be eaten when immature; in young stages they somewhat resemble the meat of the coconut. When fully mature the seed is very hard, and if eaten

25

at all in this stage should be finely grated or crushed. Local names: *Nipa, ipah, saripi, parénga, dimor, látaf, sanénem, híra, wéra, sóng, kopére, támu, bóbo, bobóro, salípi.*

SECTION VIII

EDIBLE GRASSES

■ **17. GRASSES IN GENERAL.**—*a.* To this family belong all of our cultivated cereals, such as rice, wheat, barley, oats, rye, millet, sorghum, maize or corn, etc. Rice, millet, sorghum, maize, and several other cereals are extensively cultivated in the Tropics, but one does not find rye, wheat, oats, and other cereals so characteristic of the temperate regions. The bamboos are all grasses, and the young shoots of most of these (and there are many kinds in Malaya) may be cooked and eaten with safety (see par. 18c). The cultivated sugarcane is a grass. Its juice is rich in sugar, and thus has considerable food value. A wild species of sugarcane, a coarse. harsh-leafed grass 4 to 10 feet high, or even taller in rich soil, is very common and widely distributed in open valley lands. The flower-bearing parts are white, and make the species very conspicuous. It sometimes occupies large areas and scarcely needs a description. This is known as *taláhib, gelágah, glágah, káso, tébu-sála, tatébau, tebiu, tigbau, bógang, klágah, tlengát, kénu, sáraw, hépu, dalína, djódo,* and *siuhu.* The hearts of the young shoots are frequently eaten raw or cooked, and are even sold in the markets of Java. The very young flowering parts, while still inclosèd in the upper leaf-sheaths, may be cooked and eaten, while the roots may be peeled and eaten and taste somewhat sweet like the cultivated sugarcane.

b. Some of the wild grasses allied to millet, such as our common barnyard grass, have fairly large seeds, and these are produced in abundance; they may be gathered, the seeds rubbed out of the chaff, and either boiled or roasted. While the seeds of the wild grasses are much smaller than those of our cultivated cereals, nevertheless they are perfectly safe to eat, and are actually used by the natives in times of food shortages. (See figs. 17 and 18.)

26

FIGURE 16.—Job's tears (*Coix lachryma-jobi*).

■ 18. SPECIFIC GRASSES.—*a. Job's tears* '(*Coix lachryma-jobi*).—This is coarse grass, usually 2 to 3 feet high, often abundant in open places, never found in forests. The very hard, white, shining "fruit" contains one to several fairly large seeds which may be eaten raw, boiled, or roasted. There is one form (déle, jélai, sálea, lahja, hadjeli, inúle, sáli, sári, róre, lóre), with very thin-walled brownish "fruits," frequently cultivated for its seeds. Local names: *Ádlai, kudlásan, jélai, jélai-bátu, andjálai, sũla, sána-sána, sánga-sánga, bílen, pú-pú, maniú-niu, perára, sálea-útan, hadjére,*

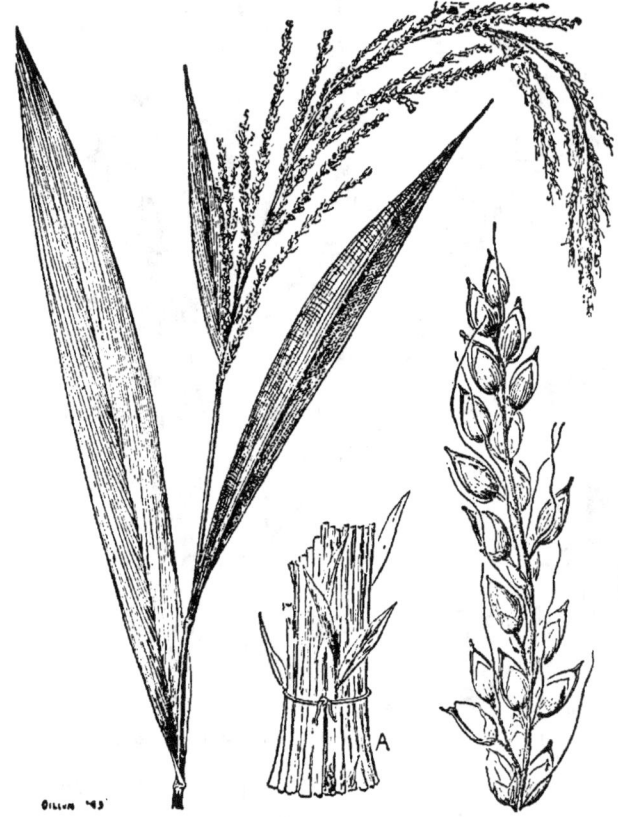

FIGURE 17.—*Setaria palmifolia.*

bukéhang, tataókok, tie, lóle, báree, kalíde, karísi, klúmba, gélem, sálea, takókok.

b. *Setaria palmifolia.*—This is a coarse grass, 2 to 6 feet high, with broad, prominently nerved leaves and very numer-

ous flowers.   It is usually abundant in old clearings, partly
shaded ravines, old plantations, and along forest borders.
The hearts of the young shoots or stout plants ((A), fig. 17)
may be eaten raw or cooked, and these are often sold in the

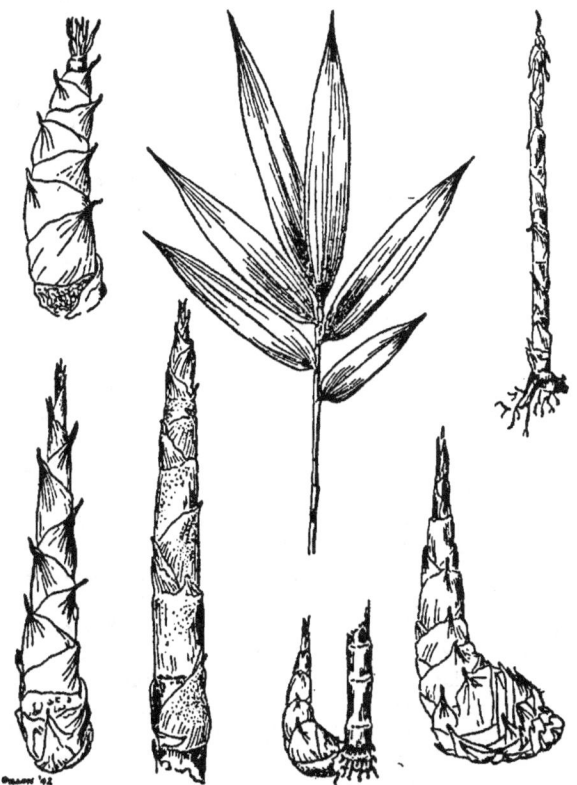

FIGURE 18.—Bamboo shoots (several types).

native markets of Java. The very numerous small seeds (the
species being allied to Italian millet) may be gathered and
boiled or roasted; these are used as a famine food in the
Philippines and elsewhere. Local names: *Lulúwan-kébo,*

29

tjewéhan, sahúen, yang-meyángan, wulúhan, lintabueng, jang-ujángan, mesé-mae, lákar, ésa-ésa, wáru-wári, sówa-sowáne, agusáis, asáhas, hagusáis, dúmbug.

    c. Types of bamboo shoots.—There are many different kinds of bamboo in Malaysia and a few in Polynesia. They occur often in great abundance in the open country and in the jungles and forests. The young shoots appear from near the bases of the older stalks and their growth is very rapid. All of them may be cooked and eaten when young, although in a few species the shoots are too bitter to be palatable. The surrounding, often hairy sheaths, are removed and the more or less tender inner parts are cut into small pieces and boiled, or the whole shoot may be roasted.

SECTION IX

EDIBLE TUBERS

■ 19. EDIBLE TUBERS.—*a. Sweet potato (Ipomoea batatas).*— The sweet potato is widely cultivated throughout the Old World Tropics as a staple article of food. It may be identified by its pink flowers or the shape of its leaf. In addition to the edible tubers (these may be eaten raw or cooked), *the young shoots and leaves make an excellent pot herb or substitute for spinach.* Local names: *Kamóte, kumára, úbi-djáwa, batáta, petátas, gádong, gádung, éba, piek, kepíleu, gówi, katíla, ketéla, keséla, kasténa, kastéla, piláoe, pélo, téla, sábhrang, hiwu-djáwa, watáta, báge, atetéla, wui-tútu, úwi, láme-djáwa, kandóra, úfi-sina, sáne, nom-métai, bloíni, úru, úrlau, úwi-kastéla, mángat, dáso, ránso, múe, sabakrúwa, ningoi, káv, gúmi, gumíni, bówon, íma, kápu.*

FIGURE 19.—Sweet potato (*Ipomoea batatas*).

b. Cassava, manioc, or tapioca (*Manihot esculenta*).—A plant widely cultivated in the Old World Tropics and is the commercial source of tapioca. It is a shrubby plant 3 to 5 feet high. The large roots are rich in starch. *Warning:* The two varieties, *bitter cassava* and *sweet cassava* cannot be distinguished by any characteristic other than by taste. *Bitter cassava is poisonous when eaten raw.* Cooking elimi-

31

FIGURE 20.—Cassava, manioc, or tapioca (*Manihot esculenta*).

nates the poisonous principle (*in this case hydrocyanic acid*), *but with bitter cassava it is best to crush the root thoroughly and wash the starchy mass with several changes of water. Never eat bitter cassava raw, but only after it has been thoroughly cooked.* Local names: *Kamóte-káhoy, kásbi, kaśawe, mandióka, manióta, manóka, manióta-aipi, mendióka, úfi-laáu, yúka, ufilaáu, ébae, kikóhak, ketíla, gádung-*

FIGURE 21.—Greater yam (*Dioscorea alata*).

káoe, úbi-inggris, úbi-kádju, batáta-káju, bistúngkel, húwi-dangdeur, sámpeu, tjápeu, kasápen, kasíbi, kásbi, kaspíni, káspe, ketela-pung, sikong, ménjok, sáwi, mandarási, pangála, tasíbie.

c. *Greater yam* (*Dioscorea alata*).—This is a twining vine, common in cultivation, and sometimes growing wild. The stems are ridged or with narrow wings. The yams vary

33

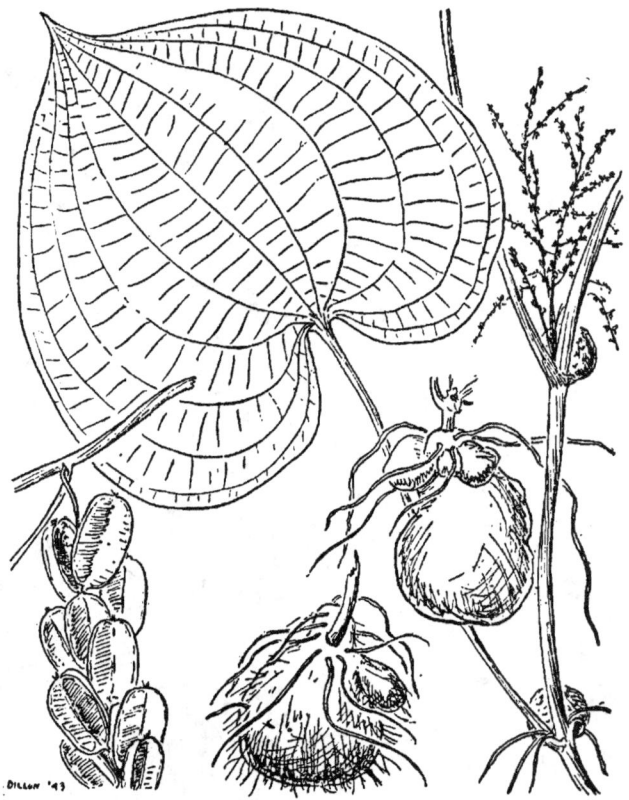

FIGURE 22.—Bulb yam (*Dioscorea bulbifera*).

enormously in shape and size, sometimes rather small, sometimes weighing up to 30 pounds. The flesh varies from white to purple. An excellent food boiled or roasted. Local names: *Úbi, úhi, úfi, úi-párai, úvi, úwi, húwi, héri, héli, láme, lútu, gúsu, dágo.*

d. Bulb yam (Dioscorea bulbifera).—This twining vine has smooth stems. It grows in thickets, and is sometimes cultivated. Usually fairly large, round, rather hard bulbs are in the leaf axils. *Warning:* While the axillary bulbs and the yams may be eaten when properly prepared (see *g* below), *they should never be eaten unprepared, as they are definitely poisonous.* Seek the advice of informed natives if possible as to how the tubers should be treated. Local names: *Húwi, búwah, gembólo, kambúbu, ahúhu, ohúhu, kapúpu, pulúgan, hói, vi, sói, abaráka, váti, nám.*

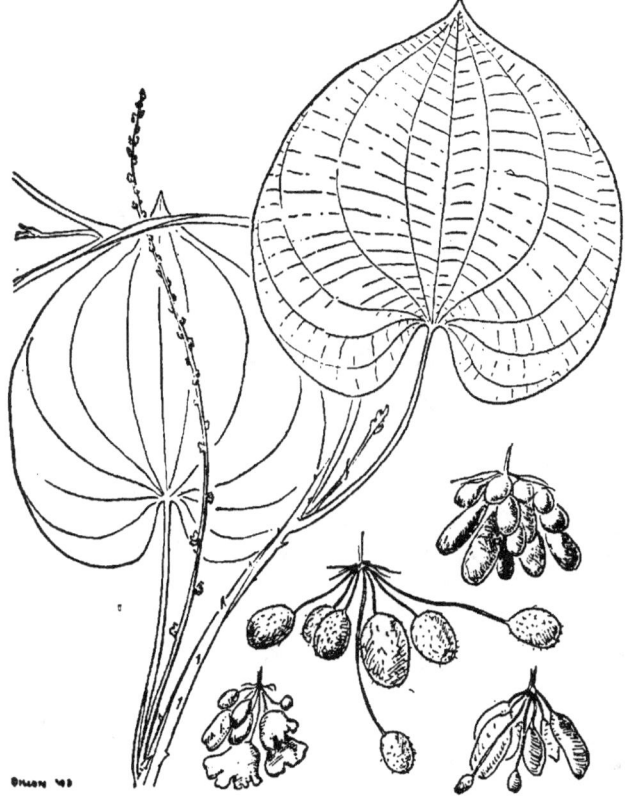

FIGURE 23.—Goa yam (*Dioscorea esculenta*).

e. Goa yam (Dioscorea esculenta).—This spiny and twining vine is cultivated, also often found wild in thickets. The

35

yams vary in shape but are usually not very large. They are distinctly well flavored, and may be eaten boiled or roasted. Like those of the greater yam they need no special treatment, as they are never poisonous. Local names: *Gembólo, gembeéli, súdo, kabúran, húwi-lándak, káwai, túgi, túngo, dágo, hoi-tía, níka, sáhu, siáju, siápu, siáwu, sajáwu, kapúgu, isáhu.*

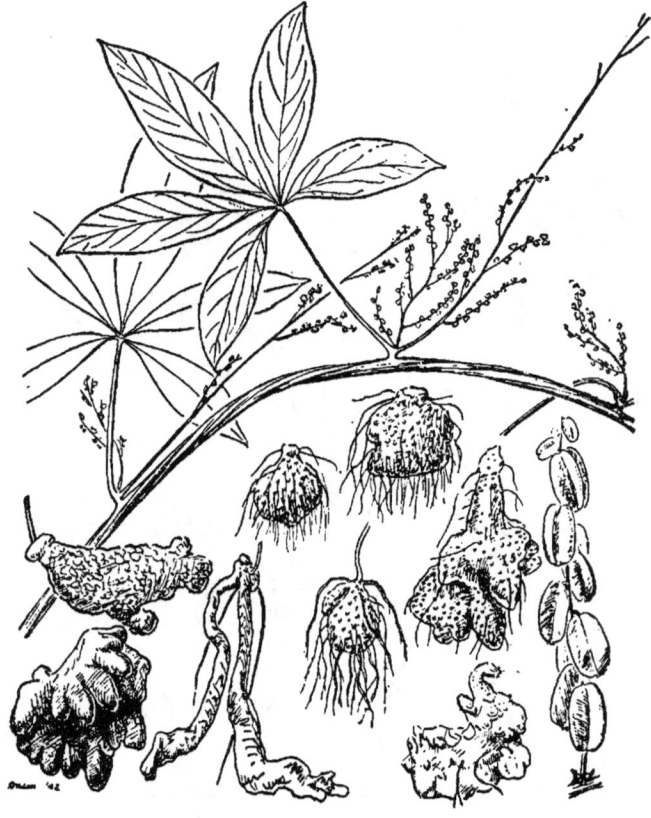

FIGURE 24.—BUCK YAM (*Dioscorea pentaphylla*).

f. Buck yam (Dioscorea pentaphylla).—This is a climbing, twining vine, the leaves usually with five parts, the stems smooth or with short scattered spines. It is sometimes cultivated, but more commonly found wild in thickets. Sometimes there are small bulbs in the leaf axils. The yams vary in shape and are usually not very large. They may be eaten boiled or roasted. Local names: *Úbi-pásir, úbi-súnda,*

FIGURE 25.—Wild yam (*Dioscorea hispida*).

37

kátak, húwi-pútri, susúan, rábet-soséan, páa, pilíta, piríta, patóra, paauára, útau, lima-lima, sápong.

g. Wild yam (Dioscorea hispida).—This is a climbing, rather woody, spiny vine; the leaves have three parts. It usually grows wild in thickets, and is rarely cultivated. The yams vary considerably in shape and size. *Warning: These yams are definitely poisonous and should not be used for food unless properly prepared;* seek the advice of natives whenever possible. *The yams should be cut into very thin slices,*

FIGURE 26.—Arrowroot (*Maranta arundinacea*).

coated with ashes if possible, and then soaked in streams or in salt water for 3 or 4 days, after which they should be dried in the sun. After prolonged treatment they may be cooked and eaten, but great caution is necessary. Local names: *Námi, gadóong, húwi-gadgóong, kápak, gádu, sikápa, bitúle, siápa, bóti, léi, hajúle, hajúru, kálut, kórot, kúlut, uále, káwai, hói-tía, nika.*

h. *Arrowroot (Maranta arundinacea)*.—This is an erect, smooth, branched herb, 1 to 3 feet high, with small white flowers. The thickened scaly roots may be cooked and eaten, or they may be crushed, the abundant starch washed out, and used as food. This is the commercial arrowroot, and is found only in cultivation. Local names: *Aráru, aréroo, arúru, ároot, angkrik, árus, djilárut, evérut, gáerut, gárut, irut, lárut, ngárut, salárut, parúta, ságu, ságu-bánban, ságurárut, pátat-ságu, táwang, húla-móa, húda-súla, péda-péda, pia, pi-walánda, lábia-walánda, masóa-jánau, tiáre-arúra.*

i. *Yam bean (Pachyrhizus erosus)*.—This vine has blue flowers. It is often common in thickets and hedgerows, and is sometimes planted. The turnip-shaped root is very refreshing, the flesh is crisp and pleasant to the taste; it is always eaten raw, never cooked. The very young pods may be cooked and eaten like string beans. *Warning: The mature seeds in brown pods should never be eaten as these are poisonous.* Local names: *Hikamas, sinkamas, bakúwang, bangkówan, bangkúwa, bangkúwang, bingkówang, bengkúwang, singkúwang, huivi-híris, besúsu, djempirángan, úbiplisak, oéas, oéa.*

j. *Polynesian arrowroot (Tacca leontopetaloides)*.—This is a plant that grows 2 to 5 feet high having stems that are distinctly grooved. The hard, usually round, and potatolike tubers are rich in starch and may be boiled or roasted and eaten, or better, crushed or grated and then boiled. *Warning: The tubers should never be eaten raw as they are said to be poisonous until after being crushed, washed, and cooked.* Usually the tubers are found in the loose soil some distance from the base of the plant and from one to several to a plant. It is sometimes cultivated, but as a wild plant is most often found in loose sandy soil not far from the seashore. Local names: *Gáu-gáu, panarien, tayóbong, ketjóndang, katjúnda,*

*tjóndang, lábing, léki, léker, likir, táka-laut, tatóan, kolo-
pále, katjódo, katjúnda, katéo, télo, táa, húda-koráno, pía,
yábia, yámbia, mára, másoa, maaéúa, mok-mok, gab-gab,
vátia, yovóli.*

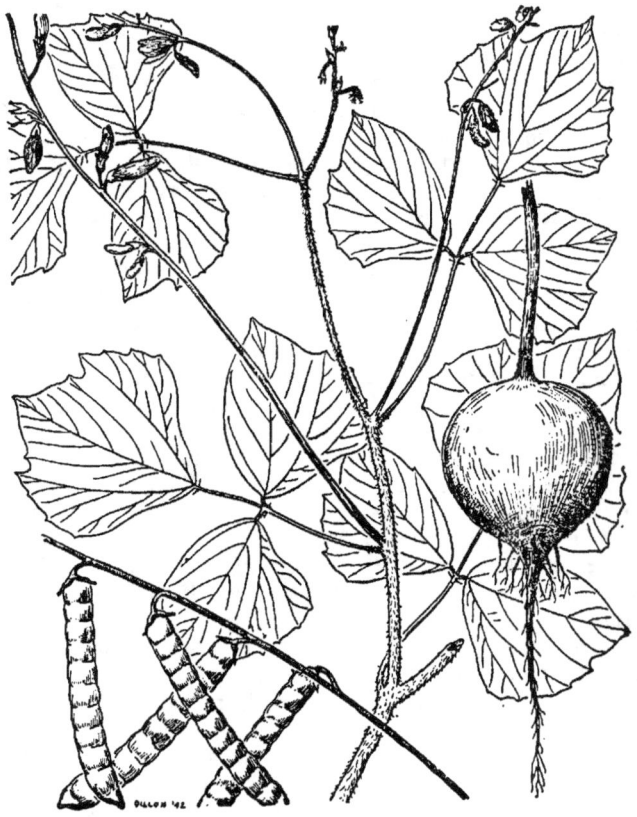

FIGURE 27.—Yam bean (*Pachyrhizus erosus*).

k. Water chestnut (Eleocharis dulcis).—This is a coarse,
more or less tufted plant, 2 to 4 feet high, growing only in
fresh water swamps in open places. The nearly round, hard
tubers are produced underground and are excellent to eat,

boiled or roasted. This is the wild form of the so-called *ma-tai* of the Chinese and the tubers in normal times are extensively imported into the United States by them and are served in Chinese restaurants. Local names: *Apúlid,*

FIGURE 28.—Polynesian arrowroot (*Tacca leontopetaloides*).

pótok, tike, tíkai, dékeng, pangóke, teréke, góro, pagóro, bigáu, mansíro-bólong, útu-útu, uchága-láhe.

41

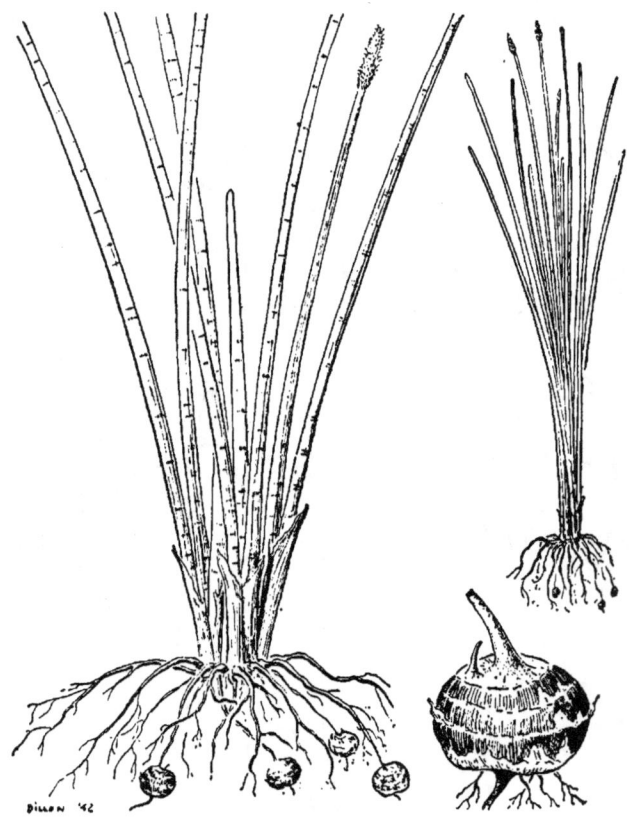

FIGURE 29.—Water chestnut (*Eleocharis dulcis*).

SECTION X

PLANTS EATEN AS GREENS

Paragraph

Plants which may be eaten as greens_____ 20

FIGURE 30.—*Luffa cylindrica, L. acutangula.*

■ 20. PLANTS WHICH MAY BE EATEN AS GREENS.—*a. A, Luffa cylindrica, B, Luffa acutangula.*—These vines are cultivated, and also often grow wild. The flowers are yellow. The young

green fruits (not more than half ripe) may be cooked and
eaten; at this stage they make an excellent vegetable; the
tender shoots, flowers, and young leaves may also be cooked
and eaten. The mature fruits are too tough to eat. One species ((A), fig. 30) has sharply angled fruits, the other (B)
has smooth fruits suggesting a smooth cucumber. The fruits
of the wild form, occurring in thickets especially near the
sea, are smaller than those of the cultivated forms. Local
names: *Patóla, petóla, ketóla, béstru, bléstru, motini, pachó-*

FIGURE 31.—Balsam vine (*Momordica charantia*).

44

dag, djingi, ójong, petóla-benggála, petóla-pándjang, petóla-tjina, kimput, émes, kátjur, húrung-djáwa, timput, lópang, dódahála, ojong.

b. *Balsam vine (Momordica charantia).*—This is a slender vine with small yellow flowers. The rough fruits, variable in shape, are usually yellow, the pulp reddish. The young leaves and shoots may be eaten as greens (better mixed with other plant material, as they are rather bitter), while the fruits may be cooked and eaten. This plant is found both in cultivation and wild; the fruits of the wild form are always smaller than are those of the cultivated ones, which may be 6 inches long or even more. Local names: *Papári, pepáre, páre, pária, pália, pánia, púlia, péria, papariáno, taparipóng, karaiáno, pariáne, paliak, peniu, pepáreh, pája, trúwuk, kámbeh, popári, fória, apaláya, ampaláya, apália, amargóso, almagóso, márgoso, pupurúvi.*

c. *Commelinaceae.*—Figure 32 shows two common and widely distributed representatives of *Cyanotis* (A) (D) and two of *Commelina* (B) (C). These are somewhat fleshy, trailing or ascending herbs, with blue flowers. They occur in open places, waste and cultivated lands and meadows, and all are common. The plants may be eaten raw, steamed, or boiled. Local names: *Brambángan, géwor, petúngan, táli-kórang, táli-sáit, rébha-mósor, alibángon, sabílau, ulikbángon, nemeneakóri, váte, mau-u-tóga, aihére-pápe, rébhakongong.*

d. *Forrestia marginata.*—This erect plant grows to about 2 feet in height. The stems are smooth or hairy with dense heads of small violet or purple flowers in the leaf axils. The tender shoots may be cooked and eaten, these parts of the plant being even sold in native markets in Malaya. Local names: *Arigbángon, táhig-táhig, limpúngan, géwor, kérokbátok.*

e. *Three species of Amaranthus.*—Various species of Amaranthus occur (often in great abundance) throughout the Malaysian and Polynesian regions, particularly in open places (especially (B) fig. 34), waste lands about settlements (especially (C)), and more or less cultivated (A). Some ((A) and (B)) are often 3 feet high; others (C) are usually

45

not more than 1 foot high. In the cultivated forms the leaves are often variegated, dull purple to even red. The young shoots and leaves of all kinds of *Amaranthus* make

FIGURE 32.—*Commelinaceae.*

excellent greens when cooked. Local names: *Kolitis, hálon, bájam, bája, bájem, váte, dríti, nakéke, dámu-dámu, árum, árun, hówa, hajóem, tárnak, tárnjak, lémbain, nádu, médja, wáwa, sinúe, sinahúe, pódo, malábut, láhut, matáhut, mala-húto, uta-paine, ut-lábut, lóda, lóda-kohóri.*

FIGURE 33.—Forrestia marginata.

f. Celosia argentea.—This ((A), fig. 35) is a wild form of the common garden cock's comb and is often abundant in meadows, old clearings, waste places, but always in the open, never in forests. It is about 2 feet high and the flower bearing parts are shining white to pink. The young shoots and leaves are boiled and eaten as greens. The garden forms of

DRAWN '42   A   B   C

FIGURE 34.—Amaranthus (three species).

the common cock's comb ((B) and (C)) may also be so used, the floral parts being red, purple, or yellow, but these forms are usually not found wild. Local names: *Borótjo, sangśri, kúntha, kindayóhan, kudiápa.*

g. *Alternanthera sessilis.*—This is a common, widely dis-

FIGURE 35.—*Celosia argentea.*

tributed, weedy plant, more or less ascending. It is found in waste places, old rice paddies, along streams and ditches, roadsides, about dwellings, in gardens, and in damp meadows.

49

It has small heads of white flowers in the leaf-axils; the leaf-form is variable. The younger parts of the plant may

FIGURE 36.—*Alternanthera sessilis.*

be cooked and eaten as greens. Local names: *Daun-rúsa, daun-tólod, kerémak, tólod, létah-háyam, bónga-bónga, vao-sosólo.*

  h. Ceylon spinach (Basella rubra).—This fleshy, twining

vine grows in hedges and along fences.   Sometimes it is cultivated.   The rather fleshy stems may be dark red, purple,

FIGURE 37.—Ceylon spinach (*Basella rubra*).

or yellowish green and the leaves may be green, red, or purplish.   It does not occur in the forest but chiefly near settlements.   The small flowers are pink and the fruits black or dark purple.   The whole plant may be eaten raw or cooked. Local names: *Libáto, arogbáti, alugbáti, dundúla, gandóla, gendóla, kendóla, gendjérot, kandóla.*

51

i. Pilea glaberrima.—This erect plant, a somewhat juicy herb, grows 2 to 5 feet high. It has opposite leaves and numerous small greenish or greenish white flowers. A number of closely allied species occur, often in great abundance, in wet or damp high forests, in shaded ravines, and along

FIGURE 38.—*Pilea glaberrima.*

streams, but always in the forest. In Java the tender young leaves and stems are eaten both raw and cooked, and are actually sold in the native markets. Local names: *Pohpóhan, tiotiok-búba* (in Java).

52

j. Purslane (Portulaca oleracea).—This very fleshy weed-like plant is often abundant in settled areas throughout the Tropics, while other forms occur near the sea. The whole

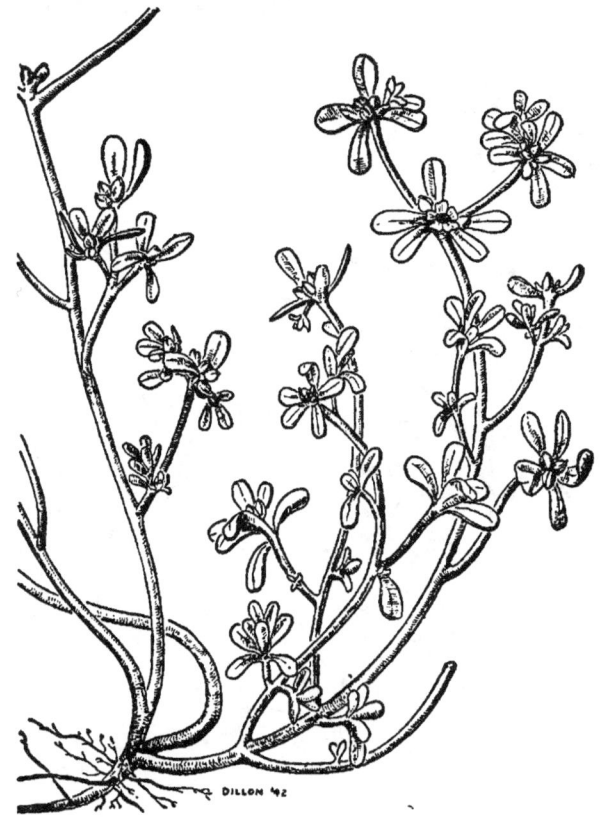

FIGURE 39.—Purslane (*Portulaca oleracea*).

plant may be eaten raw or cooked as greens. Local names: *Golasiman, ulisiman, gélang, atúri, tamóle, krókut, reseréjan, djálu-djálu-kiki.*

k. Seaside purslane (Sesuvium portulacastrum).—This is a trailing branched herb with fleshy stems and leaves, occurring only back of the beach or brackish marshes along the shores of lagoons, etc., within the influence of salt or brackish water. Widely distributed in all tropical countries. The whole plant may be eaten raw or cooked as greens, but

FIGURE 40.—Seaside purslane (*Sesuvium portulacastrum*).

it is desirable to change the water two or three times to eliminate the salt. Local names: *Chára, dampálit, gélang-láut, geláng-pasir, rúmput-bábi, kémel, djálo-djálo, tatála-dogóto, birbíri.*

l. Boerhaavia diffusa.—This is a rather diffuse, spreading or ascending, branched herb with small pink flowers, the stems often reddish or purplish. Common in open places especially near the seashore back of the beach. The somewhat thickened leaves and young somewhat fleshy stems

FIGURE 41.—*Boerhaavia diffusa.*

may be cooked and eaten. The roots are reported as being eaten in Fiji in times of scarcity, but as their use as food affects the kidneys, they should be used with caution if at all. Local names: *Katúri, máve, rima, dajóe, kisi, kalisi-lisi, rúna, rúna-rúna, múna-múna.*

m. Solanum nigrum.—This is an erect, branched herb that
normally grows 1 to 2 feet high. It has small white flowers
and small black berries. It is common both in waste places
and cultivated lands. The young leafy shoots make excellent

DILLON 42

FIGURE 42.—*Solanum nigrum.*

greens when cooked, and are extensively so used in the Tropics
of both hemispheres. The small black fruits are edible.
Local names: *Ánti, rámpai, ránti, leúntja, leúntja-bádak,
leúntja-hájam, leútja-páhit, kónti, búse, bobóse, magálo,
popólo.*

n. Ipomoea aquatica.—This vine grows only in shallow fresh water ponds and swamps, and resembles the sweet-potato vine. It has pink flowers. The tender stems and young leaves make very excellent greens, and are frequently

FIGURE 43.—*Ipomoea aquatica.*

gathered and sold in the native markets for this purpose. Local names: *Kankóng, kangkó, kankúng, naniri, pangpúng, rúmpun, kalájau, lalidih, lára, láre, sajáha, sariókang, ponángoi, kánto, tatánggo, tánggo, ángo-dáno, káko-dáno, kingkói, kongkia, utángko, béehob, takáko, káko.*

57

o. Ottelia alismoides.—This herb has rather large, thin leaves. It grows in slow shallow streams, pools, and quiet ponds, the white flowers extending above the surface of the

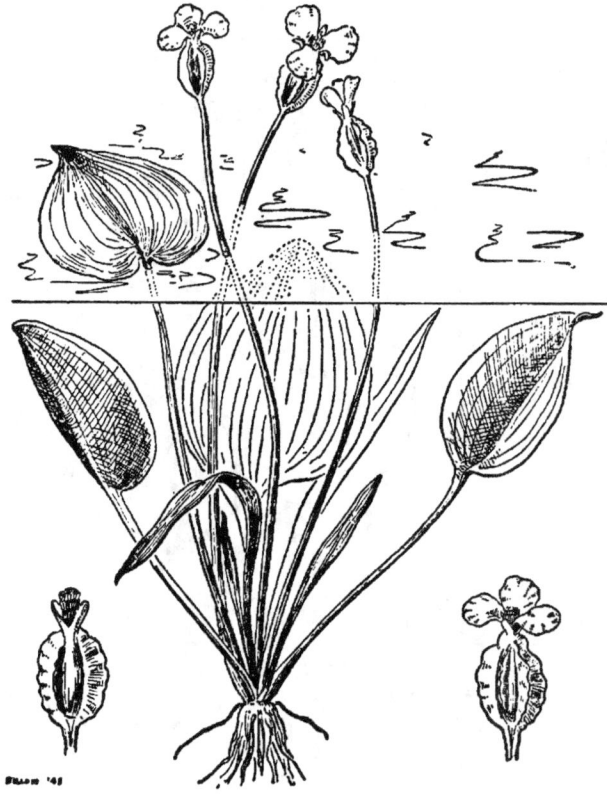

FIGURE 44.—Ottelia alismoides.

water, the leaves wholly submerged or extending to the surface. The entire plant may be cooked and eaten as greens. Local names: *Etjéng, tjowéhan, lila-lalángkow, pódang, kala-búa, dámong-ilálim, lánten-sága, tarábang.*

p. (Monochoria vaginalis and Monochoria hastata).—This herb is somewhat fleshy and grows about 1 to 1½ feét high. It grows in open wet places, old rice paddies, or along streams,

FIGURE 45.—A. *Monochoria vaginalis;* B, *Monochoria hastata.*

and is often abundant. It has blue flowers. The whole plant except the roots may be eaten raw, steamed, or boiled. Local names: *Étjeng, béngok, pingo, wewéan, étjeng-kébo, gábi-gábi, lápa-lápa, kósol-kósol.*

q. Water hyacinth (Eichhornia crassipes).—While this plant is a native of Brazil and of comparatively recent introduction in the Old World Tropics, it is now widely naturalized and wherever it occurs it is usually very abundant. The

FIGURE 46.—Water hyacinth (*Eichhornia crassipes*).

flowers are blue with a yellow spot. They float on ponds and slow streams, and also occur as a weed in rice paddies. In Malaya the young leaves, leaf stalks, and flowering parts are steamed or boiled and eaten. Local names: *Béngok, wewéan, etjeng-góndok, riri-vái.*

60

r. Emilia sonchifolia.—This is a common and widely distributed weed and usually grows less than 1 foot high. It is found in open places, meadows, wastelands, and coconut plantations, but not in the forest. The flowers are pink or

Dillon '42

FIGURE 47.—*Emilia sonchifolia.*

in some forms, reddish. The whole plant may be eaten raw or cooked. It is botanically allied to lettuce. Local names: *Djónge, momélan, sárop, sundilan, kemandélan, pátah-kemúdi, tagulinas, líbum, lamlampáka, fúaléle, meléni-váo.*

s. Erechtites.—These two weeds are very abundant in deserted clearings and waste places. *Erechtites valerianifolia*

((A), fig. 48) bears pink flowers; *Erechtites hieracifolia* (**B**), yellowish flowers. The plants are usually 2 to 3 feet high. The tender parts may be cooked and eaten as greens. Local names: *Djilámpang, púyung, bagéeni, bolóstrok, djámbrong, dóblang, koroyóno, sintróng.*

FIGURE 48.—*Erechtites.*

t. Spilanthes acmella.—This weedy herb grows both erect or ascending. It is branched and bears yellow flowers. The plant grows abundantly in meadows, waste places, along paths, in abandoned agricultural lands, but not in the forests.

The younger parts of the plant may be cooked and eaten as greens. Local names: *Dáun-gétang, dáun-gúlang, dáun-moórit, glétang, gétang, gátang, gúlang, djótang, legétan,*

FIGURE 49.—*Spilanthes acmella.*

legétan-kébo, sarúnen, sarúnei-sápi, srúnen, djótjong, djótjong-sáwa, kirat-tjirat, rát-tjirat, bága, gatáng-gátang, pilat-pilat. dáun-láda.

    u. Pluchea indica.—This small shrub grows 2 to 3 feet high. It is common and widely distributed, especially near the seashore and in wet soil. It bears a pale violet flower.

The young leaves, tips of the branches, and young flowers may be cooked and eaten, and are extensively so used in Java. Local names: *Beluñtas, luñtas, tluñtas, baluñtas, baruñtas, bluñtas, lamutása, lenábou, nih, bañig-bañig, bañing-bañing, kalapini.*

FIGURE 50.—*Pluchea indica.*

v. Acalypha indica.—This is an erect, branched herb which grows up to 3 feet high. It occurs as a weed about settlements, in meadows, along ditches, and in waste places generally, often abundantly; it does not occur in the forests. The young leaves and tender stems may be cooked and eaten. Local names: *Lelátang, láteng-pútih, bayéman, tjéka-mas, óngo-óngo.*

w. Acalypha wilkesiana.—This is an ornamental shrub

FIGURE 51.—*Acalypha indica.*

which grows 5 to 15 feet high. It has green or reddish twigs and variegated leaves, green and variously mottled or light red, dark brownish red, sometimes with greenish-yellow blotches, or pale edges ((B), fig. 52). It is easily recognized by its colored leaves. It is a native of Polynesia and is planted in hedges and near houses throughout Malaya, frequently abundant. The young shoots and young leaves may

FIGURE 52.—*Acalypha wilkesiana.*

be cooked and eaten. There are various other species of this genus, herbs, shrubs, or small trees, all with green leaves, whose young parts may also be similarly prepared and eaten with safety. Local names: *Dáun-mángsi, dáun-nángsi, kalambúci, kalabúci-dámu.*

x. Horseradish tree (Moringa oleifera).—This is a small or medium-sized tree, 15 to 20 feet high, with fine thin leaves and white flowers.   It is cultivated and spontaneous in many parts of the Old World Tropics, but is not found in the forests.

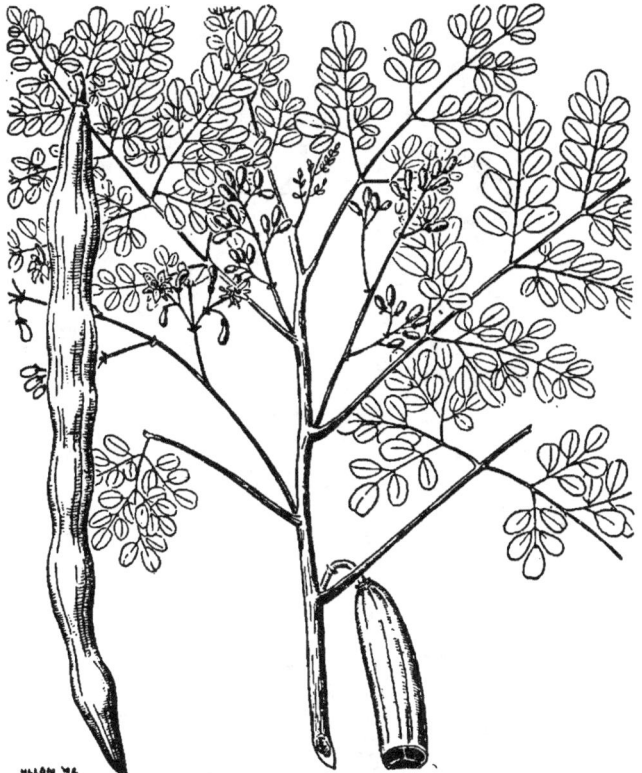

FIGURE 53.—Horseradish tree (*Moringa oleifera*).

The leaves, shoots and young pods make excellent greens when cooked, or they may be eaten raw.   The roots have the characteristic biting taste of horseradish.   The mature pods are too tough to be eaten, but the seeds may be roasted and used as food.   Local names: *Malúngai, marúngai, moúrong, remúngai, múngai, barúngai, paróngi, kélo, kélor, kelóro, kérol, kérel, kéror, kelóhe, kilor, tjélor, kawóna, wóna, móltong, wóri, kái-jok, húe-jo, pó, jók, kenéle, wakeréle, uto-keleño, uwa-kerélo.*

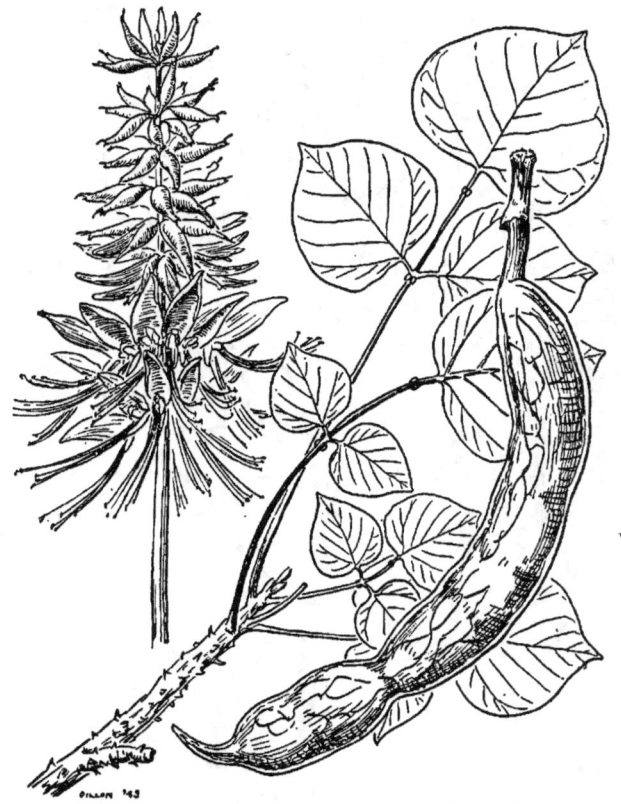

FIGURE 54.—Coral tree (*Erythrina variegata*).

y. Coral tree (Erythrina variegata).—This tree grows from 20 to 50 feet in height. It is common along the seashore, and is often planted in settled areas along roadsides. The rather large, crowded flowers are *bright red*. It does not occur in the high forest. The young branches are usually somewhat spiny. The leaves and the tender shoots may be steamed or boiled and eaten as greens. Local names: *Dáp-dap, dádap, dádap-laut, dhádhak, beléndung, théthek,*

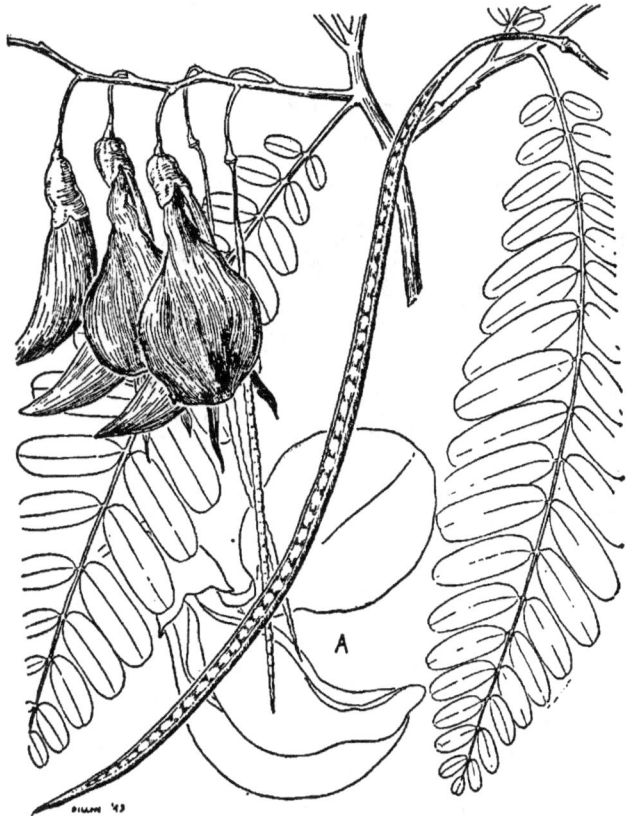

FIGURE 55.—*Sesbania grandiflora.*

déris, galála-kokótu, galála-itam oéken, lóla-kohóri, pápa-aúko, ngolóla-dalatóro, drála, álo-álo, gatáe, gáb-gab, gáp-gap, gáo-gao, isdára, rál, rár.

z. Sesbania grandiflora.—This slender tree bears long, slender, hanging pods up to 2 feet long or longer, and large white or wine-red flowers, these 2 to 3 inches long. These trees are sometimes planted and often naturalized; they are

FIGURE 56.—*Thespesia populnea.*

not in the forests. The young leaves and the young pods may be cooked and eaten, while the large flowers and flower buds are very commonly cooked and used as food. An outline of the very large flower is shown in figure 55 (A). *Do not eat the mature seeds.* Local names: *Túrí, túli, túring, tóroj, túwi, súri, paláwii, tanúnu, katúdai, ghúnga, uliángo, kála, katúri, katúrai, gáuai-gáuai, kaṁbang-túri oújai, oúai.*

aa. Thespesia populnea.—This is a small or medium sized tree bearing large yellow flowers. It is found chiefly near the seashore and usually immediately back of the beach. The smooth leaves may be eaten raw or cooked, as well as the flower buds and the flowers. The rather dry, nearly, round fruits are not edible. Local names: *Milo, miro, banáa, banálo, banágo, bálu, báru-laut, pengégen, pakeéna, amáe, váte, námir, novómil, múlo-múlo, wáru-laut, sálimúli, hálimúli.*

ab. Pemphis acidula.—This is a small tree attaining a height of 10 or 12 feet. It has small, 6-parted flowers and small leaves. It is found only along the seashore, where it is common and very widely distributed. The small leaves have a distinctly acid taste and may be eaten raw. Local names: *Ngingia, sanggále, aie, eági, gie, ngie, ingia, kónge, nigas, nigáshi, ngángae, nánghi, kasúgel, bantigi, kabantigi, pantigi, liyat, mentigi, wákat-bési, tjántiḡi, sántigi, séntigi, ménthigi, kenéas, silu-tási,*

ac. Tournefortia argentea.—This is a shrub with stout branches. It has grayish white, very hairy leaves and many small, crowded flowers. It grows only on sandy seashores, and is common and widely distributed. The leaves may be eaten raw. Local names: *Tauhúnu, tausini, tahínu, tausúnu, tahúnu, tohónu, tainu, húnik, húnig, geo-geo, sásran, néyinpóri, nánquitpára, náth, bukábuk, móral-babúlu, babaúkan, kibáko, ládu-bóling, mókal-ahúa, móral-ahúa, néla, kárpo.*

ad. Morinda citrifolia.—This is a shrub or small tree, varying from 4 or 5 to 10 or 15 feet in height. It is common along the seashore. The flowers are white and the fruits are greenish white. The young leaves and the young fruits may be eaten raw or cooked, and the mature fruits, deprived of their seeds, may also be eaten. Local names: *Bengkúdu, mengkúdu, bangkúdo, bangkúro, bakúlu, béntis, kemúdu, kúdu, pátje, tjangkúdu, kódhuk, paṁari, makúdu, manakúdu, mangkúdu, mekúdu, wangkúdu, tibah, aikómbo, eíno, ṉén, nino, nénu, túmbong-áso, nóni, nónu, láda, nácour, gógu, nóbul, malúeg, kúra, wor̃pil, alin.*

ae. Cantala (Agave cantala).—This form of the "century plant" is extensively grown in the drier parts of the Malayan region, sometimes in plantations, sometimes as scattered plants in fence rows, waste places, etc., where it is naturalized.

FIGURE 57.—*Pemphis acidula.*

The thick, fleshy leaves, 3 to 6 feet long, are very sharp-pointed and their edges are very spiny. In Java, the tender heart or "cabbage" ((A), fig. 60) in the crown of the growing plant is extensively eaten. It should be cut into small pieces and well cooked, preferably with one or two changes of water.

FIGURE 58.—*Tournefortia argentea.*

Warning: Many of the American species are not edible; some contain saponin and others contain minute stinging crystals of oxalate of lime. Seek the advice of natives whenever possible. Local names: *Nánas-kósta, nánas-sábrang, nánas-batáwi, nánas-balándah, gánas-sábrang, lánas-balándah,*

FIGURE 59.—*Morinda citrifolia.*

mágei, píta, laláto-boláno, péna-séuk, nas-wátan, nanáhi-djawa.

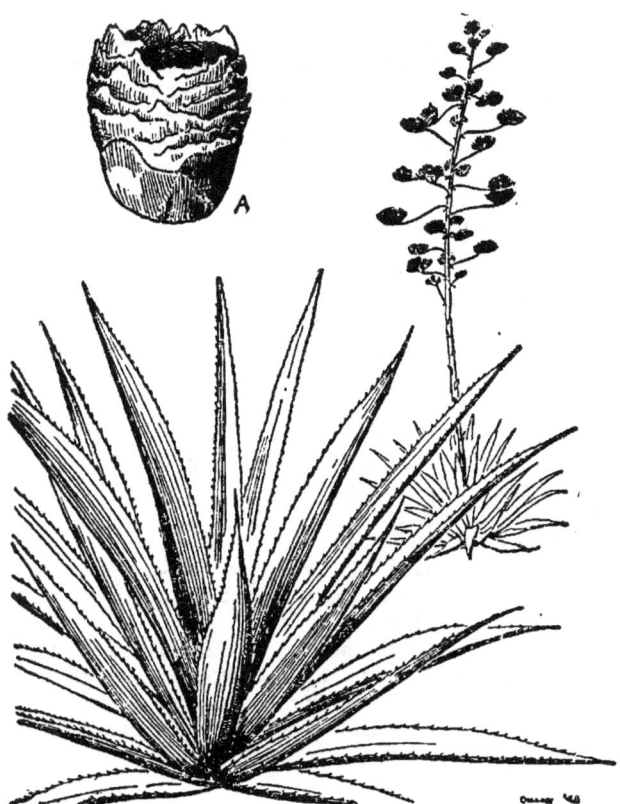

FIGURE 60.—Cantala *(Agave cantala).*

SECTION XI

EDIBLE FRUITS

■ 21. FRUITS IN GENERAL.—*a.* There are scores of varieties of the common banana, and for all practical purposes the plantain cannot be distinguished from the edible banana except that all the bananas may be eaten raw, while the plantain fruits must be cooked—either boiled, fried, or roasted; green and ripe bananas may also be cooked. The fruits vary much in shape and size as well as in color, varying at maturity from green to various shades of yellow, or even brownish-purple. Many wild forms occur in the forested regions (usually, however, not in the high forest except along streams). The fruits of the wild species contain numerous seeds and small quantities of pulp, but even these may be gathered when young and cooked. Other parts of the banana plant may be used as food, especially the fairly large more or less cone-shaped terminal flower bud (see A, fig. 61). These flower buds may be boiled or roasted in hot ashes, and certain varieties make an excellent vegetable; others contain fairly large quantities of tannic acid and are hence bitter, but the bitter principle may be eliminated in part by cooking in several changes of water. With the bitter kinds it is best to cut the bud into rather small pieces before cooking.

b. The soft inner parts of the rather thick root and the tender heart of the base of the stems may be cut into small pieces, boiled, and eaten. Even the small shoots from the lower parts of the plant may be cooked and eaten when nothing better is available.

c. In general these statements apply to all types of the banana, whether wild or cultivated. While the parts other than the fruits and the flower buds do not rate as first class food by any means, yet they are safe to eat when boiled or roasted.

■ 22. SPECIFIC FRUITS.—*a. Banana.*—This fruit is too well known to discuss here. The banana may be eaten raw or cooked, but the plantain requires cooking. Other parts of the cultivated bananas and plantains, and of the wild forms that occur in the forests and old clearings, may be boiled or roasted and eaten, especially the large flower bud ((A), fig. 61). (B) is a wild and cultivated banana extending from the Moluccas and New Guinea to Polynesia, with erect fruit clusters. There are innumerable native names for the common banana and plantain; some of those for *Musa Troglody-*

ta̱rum are: *Fei, maia, soa'a, huétu, laúfu, dáak, túngkat-lángit.*

b. *Papaw* or *Papaya* (*Carica papaya*).—This is a soft wooded, erect, normally unbranched tree.   It usually grows

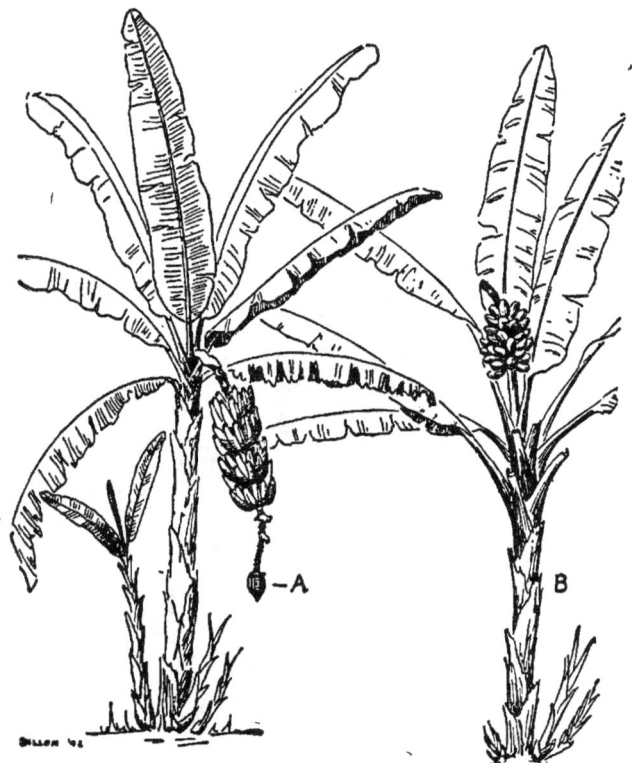

FIGURE 61.—Banana (A, *Musa sapientum;* B, *Musa troglodytarum*).

from 6 to 15 feet high.   The large yellow melonlike fruits are borne on the trunk, and are excellent food.   The green immature fruits may be cooked and eaten.   The young leaves and leaf-stems and flowers (the male flowers borne on separate plants) may be cooked and eaten as greens.   *It is, how-*

77

ever, important that such parts be cooked with several changes of water to remove the bitter taste and certain harmful substances. Local names: *Papáya, papája, popája, tapája, gédang, ési, uliti, kabaélo, pértek, pastéla, bétik,*

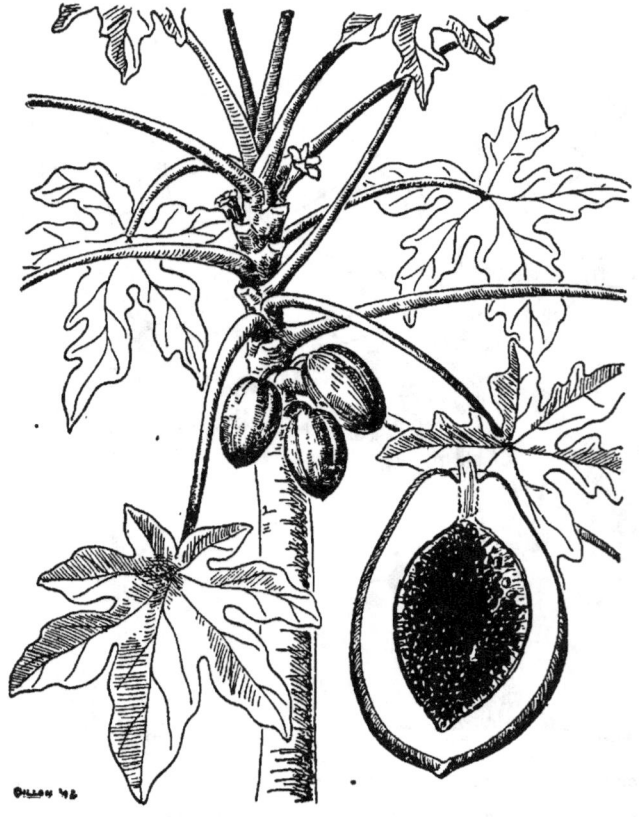

FIGURE 62.—Papaw or Papaya (*Carica papaya*).

embétik, bótik, bála, si-káilo, kátes, kahája, kehája, kapála, kustéla, nasílu, kalikih, pantjéne, mádjan, bádas, bándas, mándjan, hángo, pádu, kási, kaliki, sumojówi, titímu, mue-

mála, údi-mélai, úta-málai, paláki, sempáin, siberiáni, sám-ber, titgóno.

c. *Breadfruit (Artocarpus altilis)*.—This is a large tree that may grow 40 feet high or more. It has very large lobed

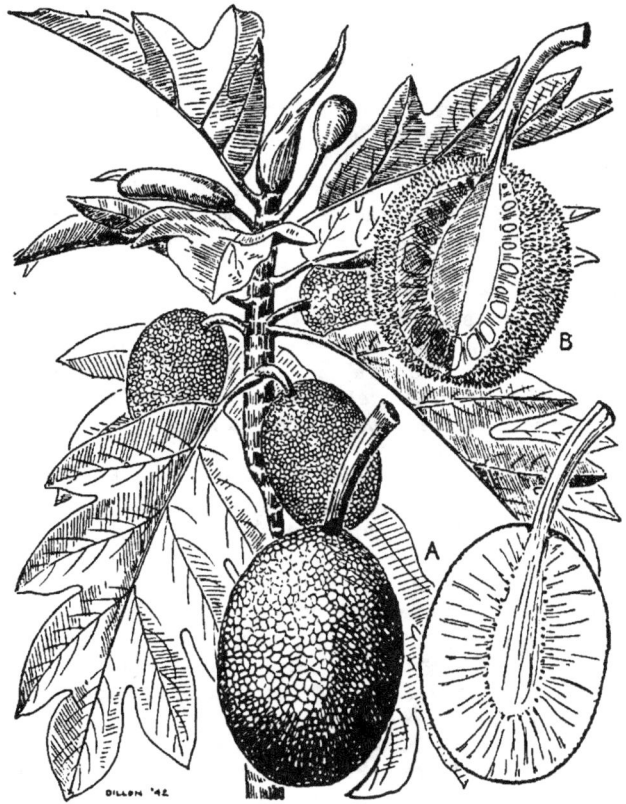

FIGURE 63.—Breadfruit *(Artocarpus altilis).*

leaves and rather large, nearly round green or brownish-green fruits. It is a basic food plant in many parts of Polynesia, where many cultivated varieties are found. The seedless form ((A), fig. 63) is utilized either boiled, baked, or fried. The large seeds in the seeded form (B) (Malaysia), boiled or roasted, are excellent food, as are the seeds of other species. Local names: *Mái, úlu, úru, úto, lémai, dúg-dug, ríma, kúru, súku, sukúen, súkon, karára, suúne, sóu, máguh, ne-máre, tháo, hatópul, kúlu, gómo, gómu, gogómo, hémo, ulúle, urúle, úlur, húkun, lákuf, kulóro, bitála, kalúweh, kemánsi, kaláwi, géi, tu, ámo, múe, ur-knam, karára, kalára, kúndu, námu, kúu.*

d. *Jak fruit* (*Artocarpus heterophylla*).—This is a large tree, normally cultivated only. The very large greenish or yellowish-green fruits are 1 to 3 feet long, and sometimes weigh up to 40 pounds. The fruits are borne directly on the tree trunk and larger branches. The pulp may be eaten raw. The numerous large seeds make excellent food when boiled or roasted. There are many different species of *Artocarpus* in Malaysia. All have abundant milky sap, and the seeds of all of them are edible when cooked. Local names: *Lángka, nángka, nángkeu, náka, nanáka, pána, pánas, panása, pinása, anásah, náa, sósak, lamása, malása, menáso, benáso, bátuk, báduk, enáduk, máduk, hóka, tjídu, naná-kang, kúlop, úlu- náka, amnaálo, taféna, náka, nákai, nákan, nakáne, náknak, anáa, anáane.*

e. *Champedak* (*Artocarpus champeden*).—This large tree has a milky sap. Its leaves are more or less hairy. The large, cylindric fruits borne on the larger branches are smaller than in the jak fruit and have a very strong odor. The pulp is edible and the seeds are edible when boiled or roasted. Local names: *Champédak, tjampédak, tuéda, bikáwan, sibódak, subódak, tembédak, temédak, tiwádak, tjapédak, kákon, pulútan, batéda, náka-wára, kawéra, kaférak, tábodóko, tewálak, nakáne, anáa-wási, ináale, taféla, ésiólo, anáane, tambérak, tuáda, tuádak.*

f. *Artocarpus rotunda.*—This large tree has a milky juice. The fruit is round, greenish or greenish brown, and is found on the smaller branches. These fruits are up to 5 inches in diameter and covered with short stiff conical spines. This tree occurs in Malaysia, but not in Polynesia. The fruit is one of the best of Malayan fruits, the well-flavored pulp being eaten raw.   The large seeds should be boiled or roasted before eating.   Local names: *Kósar, peúsar, tampúnai, tampúnik, kelédang, mandalika, púrin, táwan.*

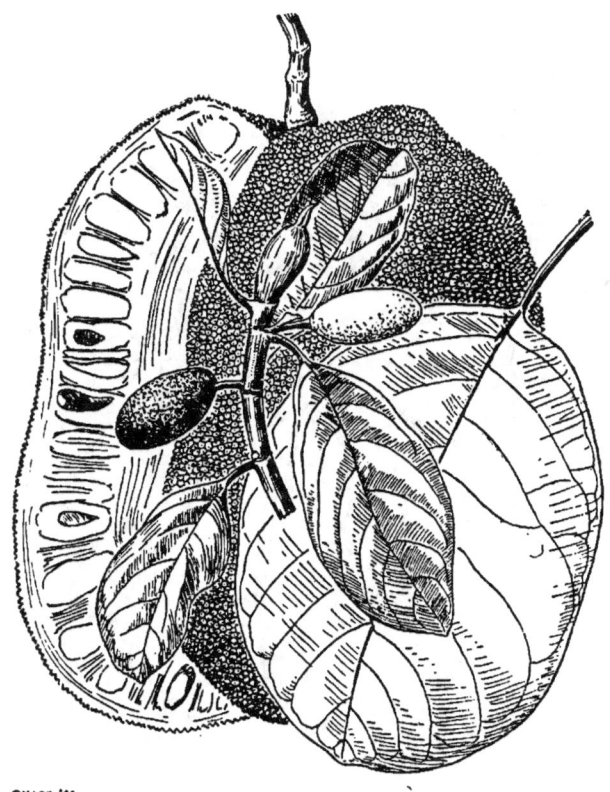

FIGURE 64.—Jak fruit *(Artocarpus heterophylla).*

g. Rambutan (Nephelium lappaceum) and Pulusan (Nephelium mutabile).—These fairly large trees are usually culti-vated, but the Pulusan is sometimes found in forests. The characteristic red fruits are one-seeded. The seed is sur-

81

rounded by a white unusually well-flavored pulp. Both the Rambutan and the Pulusan are among the very best fruits of Malaya. Local names: (A) *Rambútan, rámbot, rambúta, djaílan, sokápas, púru-biá·wak, hahújam, kakápas, líkis, síban,*

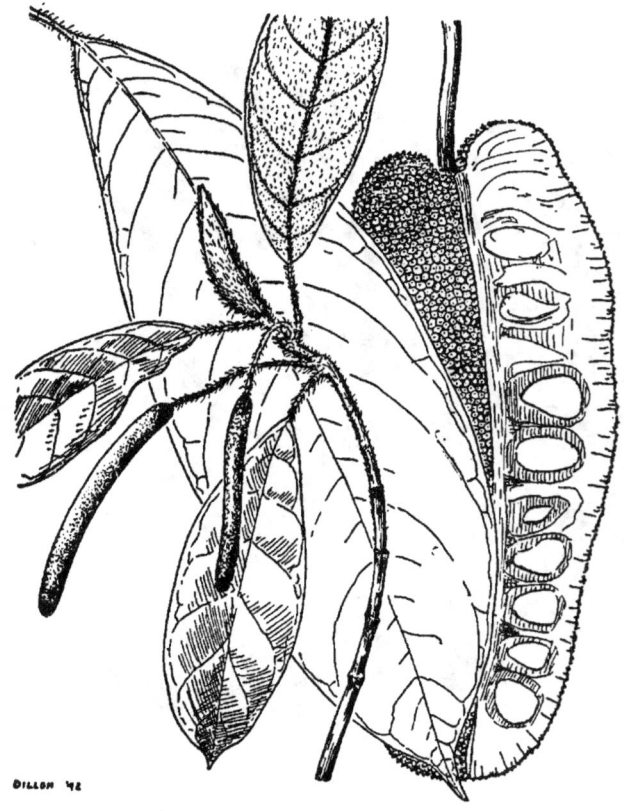

FIGURE 65.—Champedak (*Artocarpus champeden*).

biríti, sagálong, belíti, malíti, kajókan, púson, usáre, bulúwan, walátu, wajátu, balátu, lelámu, toléang; (B) *Pulúsan, pulásan, túkou-biáwak, kapulásan, mólaitómo, mulítan, báli, bulála, lintias, lagúan, potían.*

h. *Lansone (Lansium domesticum).*—This a cultivated tree.

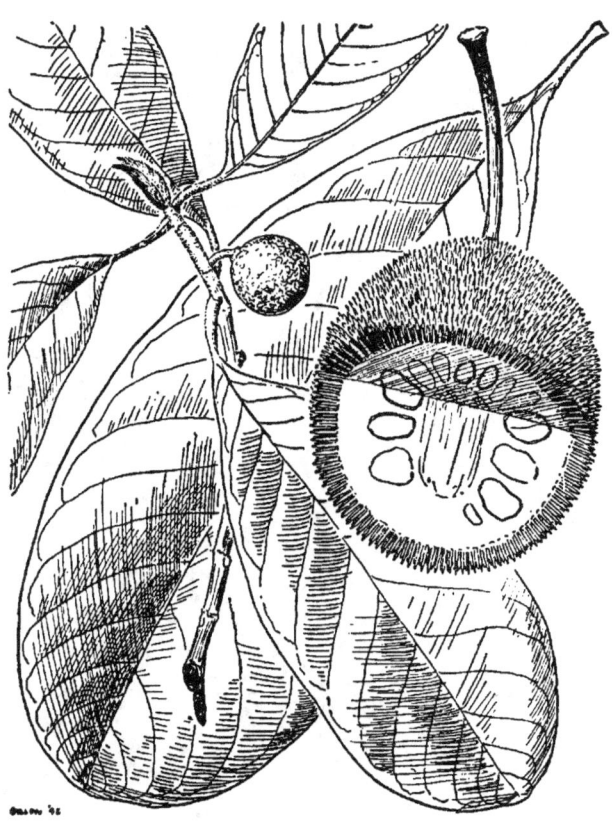

FIGURE 66.—*Artocarpus rotunda.*

The pale, yellowish fruits are found on the trunk and on the larger branches below the leaves. It is one of the best of the tropical fruits. Local names: *Lansóne, lángsat, láha, lánsa, lása, láse, lásat, lasáte, áha, rásak, ríhat, láwak, léhat, laínsa, lalátsat, lasátol, lakáole, nasáte, lángsep, tjelóring, dúku, dúkem, lúkem, lukáma, dánsot, ránso, lónsong.*

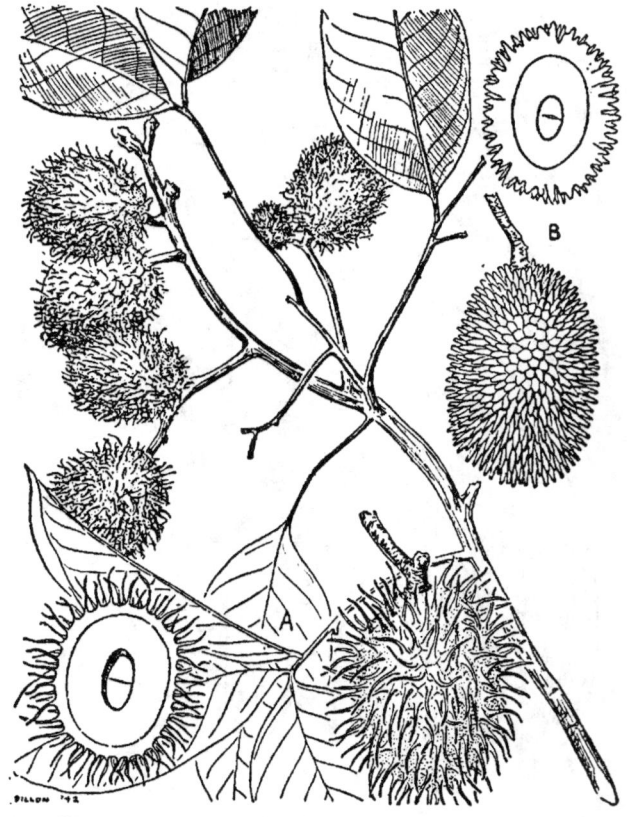

FIGURE 67.—A, Rambutan (*Nephelium lappaceum*); B, Pulusan (*Nephelium mutabile*).

i. Guava (Psidium guajava).—This is a small shrub or tree that grows 5 to 15 feet high, often abundant, but never found in real forests. It has white flowers and pale greenish or yellowish-green, smooth, many-seeded fruits.   This excellent fruit may be eaten raw or cooked.   Local names: *Bayábas, guayábas, guábang, kuáva, ábas, tuáva, biáwas, gawája,*

FIGURE 68.—Lansone (*Lansium domesticum*).

djámbu-bídji, galíman, biáwas, gogáwas, kedjáwas, piáwas, libu, bajáwas, petókal, tókal, sotong, guáwa, wajámas, kojabása, bojówat, dámbu, biabúto, kudjábas, kojábas, kajawáse, kojajáte, gawája.

j. Cashew (Anacardium occidentale).—This is a small or medium sized tree usually about 20 feet high. It is often common in more or less settled areas, but not in the forests.

FIGURE 69.—Guava (*Psidium guajava*).

The yellowish to purplish very juicy large part of the fruit is very refreshing. The single seed in the smaller part of the fruit is the cashew nut of commerce and should be eaten boiled or roasted. *Warning: The sap in the shell of the small part of the fruit surrounding the seed is very caustic. In boiling or roasting the seed-bearing part, avoid the steam or smoke.* Local names: *Balúbag, kásoi, djámbu-mónje,*

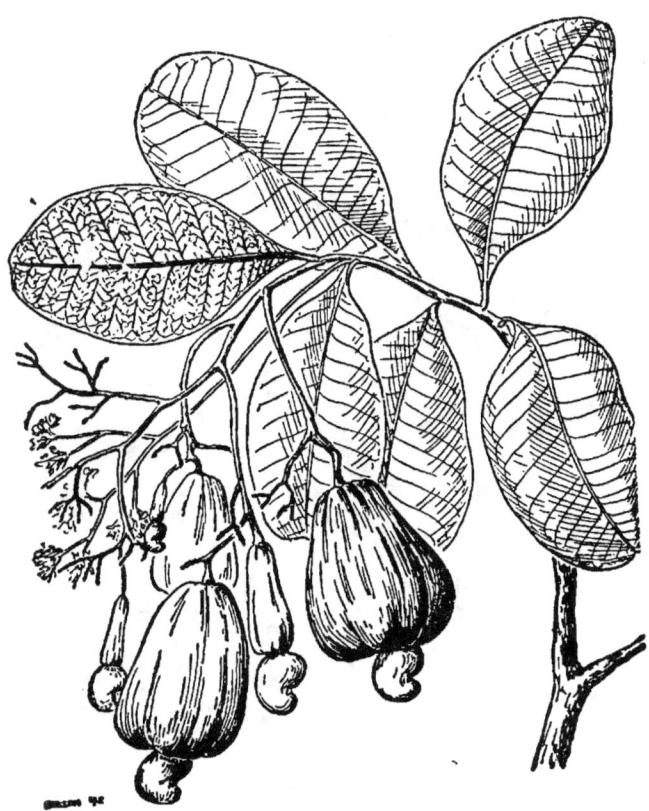

FIGURE 70.—Cashew (*Anacardium occidentale*):

djámbu-dípa, djámbu-gádjus, djámbu-érang, djámbu-síki, djámbu-méte, djámbu-dwípa, gádiu, wojákis, kanóke, mása-pána, búwa-jakía, búwah-mónjet.

87

k. Sweet sop (Annona squamosa).—This is a small tree, usually 15 feet high, and is found both wild and in cultivation. The medium-sized pale green fruit is of excellent

FIGURE 71.—Sweet sop (*Annona squamosa*).

flavor and is always eaten raw. This tree is found chiefly in and near settlements, not in the forests. Local names: *Átis, atísi, apéli, áta, sarikája, srikája, sirikája, srikáwis, sarkádja, garóso, pérse, hirikája.*

1. Sour sop (Annona muricata).—This tree is about 15 feet high, rather similar to the sweet sop, is generally cultivated, but is sometimes wild. It is found chiefly in and near settle-

FIGURE 72.—Sour sop (*Annona muricata*).

ments, not in the forests. The large, well-flavored greenish fruits are always eaten raw. Local names: *Guayábano, laguána, nángka-belánda, nángka-walánda, nángka-ma-*

89

nila, nángka, móris, dúrian-belánda, swírswak, súrsak, djámbu-lónda, srikája-djáwa, srikája-welándi, surikája-welánda, náka, nákat, haniiso, ánad-walánda, anáa-waláta, ináa-waláta, taféna-waráta.

FIGURE 73.—Custard apple (*Annona reticulata*).

m. Custard apple (Annona reticulata).—This tree, about 15 feet high, is similar to the sweet sop and the sour sop. It is found chiefly in cultivation in the settled areas, never in the forests.   The large well-flavored greenish juicy fruits are eaten raw.   Local names: *Anónas, manóna, nóna, nónas, búwah-nóna, tápu-tápu, sérba-rábsa, djámbu-nóna, djus, manówa, malówa, múlwa, kanówa, kemúlwa, klúwa, sirikája-súsu, nóna-daélok, áta-káse, boinon.*

FIGURE 74.—Mango (*Mangifera indica*).

n. Mango (Mangifera indica).—This is usually a large tree, mostly planted; not found in the forests.   It is one of the very best of tropical fruits.   Most of the varieties in Malaya and Polynesia have yellow fruits. Rarely an individual may be allergic to mangos, and in such 'cases a skin rash may develop; very rarely the individuals may be affected by the leaves. Other species of the genus in Malaya, all with edible fruits, have a very irritating sap (bínjai, báchang,

FIGURE 75.—Sapodilla (*Achras zapota*).

lánjut, kwíni) affecting the skin quite as does poison ivy. The indicated treatment is the same as for poison ivy poisoning. Local names: *Mánga, mángga, mága, páho, páo, po, mempélam, lempélam, morpólom, bálem, pégun, peígu, páger, ampélam, pélam, gúwae, áwa, lélit, wówa, páwen, rúwe, maplàne, màblang, apàlum, ajàer, balàmo, soh, ólai, taípa.*

o. *Sapodilla (Achras zapota).*—This is a medium sized tree, usually 15 to 25 feet high, with a milky sap.   It grows

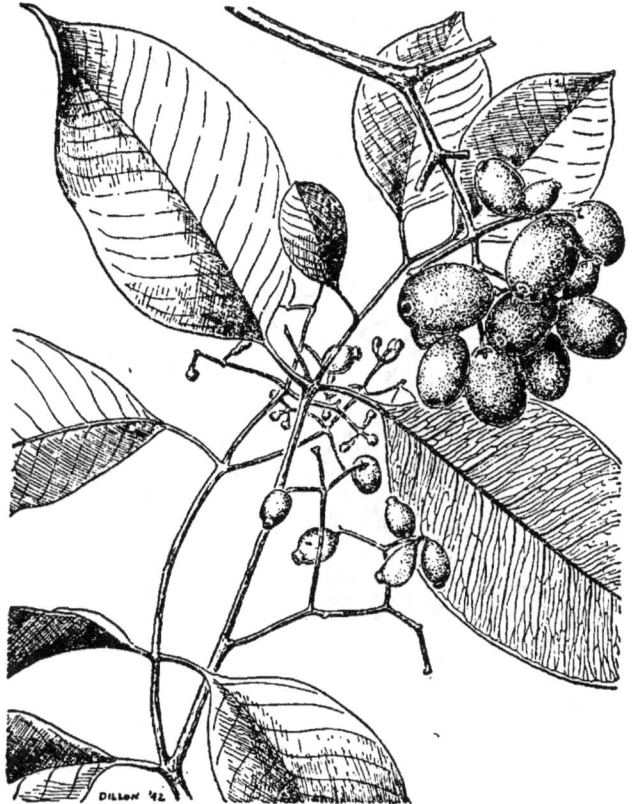

FIGURE 76.—Jambolan (*Syzygium cumini*).

both cultivated and spontaneously, but not in the forests. The grayish to brownish fruits vary in shape from round to oval and are excellent to eat.   The pulp which is pinkish-white to reddish-brown is sweet and somewhat granular. The pulp surrounds several fairly large smooth black seeds. They should not be cooked. Local names: *chico, sáwo-lónda, sábu-manéla, sába-djawa, tjiku, sáwo-manila*.

FIGURE 77.—*Syzygium aqueum*.

p. Jambolan (Syzygium cumini).—This is a medium sized tree which grows 20 to 30 feet high. It is found both wild and cultivated. The tree has somewhat leathery leaves, small white flowers, and one-seeded, light to dark purple, smooth fruits. The single seed is surrounded by a whitish or yellowish, sourish, rather pleasant tasting edible pulp. Local names: *Dúhat, djambúlang, dúwe, djambélang, djambúla, djámlang, djúwet, djiwat, dhálus, klágu.*

q. *Syzygium aqueum.*—This small tree, 15 to 20 feet high, is chiefly cultivated, but sometimes grows wild. The leaves are short-stalked and grow in opposite pairs. The flowers are white to pink in color. The edible fruits are smooth, pink in color, and somewhat juicy. *There are many different species of Syzygium in the forested regions and their fruits may be eaten with entire safety, although some have almost no pulp.* The flowers of all species are white, pink, or red, and always have many stamens. The fruits vary greatly in size, some of them being dry with no pulp, others with fairly ample pulp, which is usually acid. Local names (*S. aqueum*) : *Támbis, tábis, arbóttle, macúpa, indáhau, jámbu-áyer, jámbu-jémbir, sámba, góra, kúbal, kúmpas, jámbu-mangkóa, kumpása, kokúka, kómbas, kémbes, kébes, kéket, omúto, tákaw, gámbu, wúa-úsa, tepéte, lutúne-waéle, popóte, oúna, járem, ausáhmoh, puróri, jádi.*

r. *Malay apple (Syzygium malaccense).*—This is a medium sized tree, 15 to 30 feet high, with somewhat leathery leaves. The red flowers are found on the branches below the leaves. This tree is chiefly cultivated. The pink to reddish, thin skinned, smooth fruit, somewhat resembling an apple, varies from 2 to 4 inches in length. The thick, rather well-flavored pulp surrounding the large seed is edible. Local names: *Djámbu-bérteh, djámbu-ból, djámbu-súsu, djámbol, mangkóa, góra-mérah, góra-lámo, góra-tóme, darsána, dersána, kochúa, úpo, kúpo, koa, máku, mutíha, lutúne, nutúne, rutúno, álu, kumkólo, gogóa, gorógo, súo.*

s. *Rose apple (Syzygium jambos).*—This is a small tree, 10 to 15 feet high, and has white flowers. The fruits are somewhat rose-scented, greenish white, egg-shaped or somewhat pear-shaped and are about 1 inch long. This tree is often planted and occurs also in thickets, waste places, and secondary forests. The tree has a wide distribution. The fruits are eaten raw. Local names: *Jámbu-máwar, jámbu-*

dersána, jámbu-kelámpok, jámbu-búlu, jámbu-kráton, kóm-bot, kémbes-wolánda, kekéte, tampoi, yámpoi, kahika, kahika-papáa.

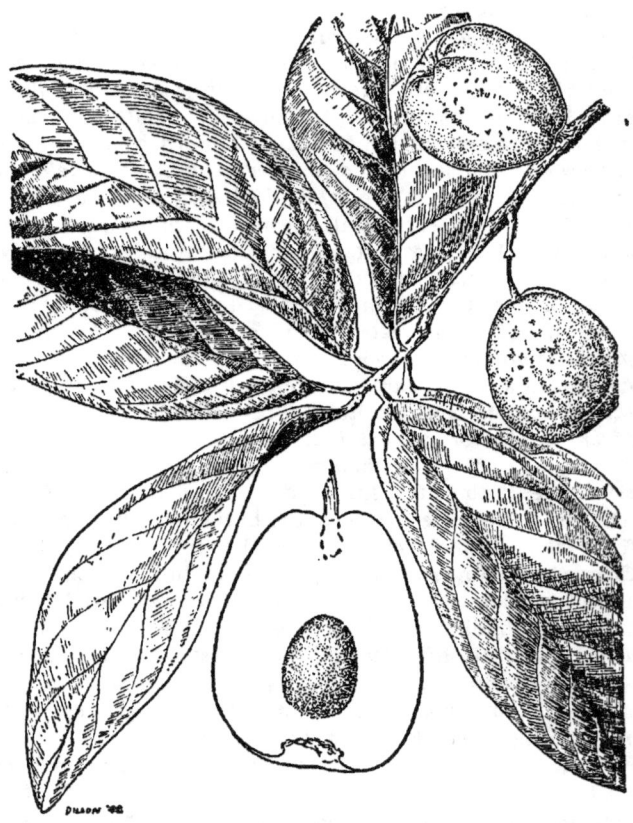

FIGURE 78.—Malay apple (*Syzygium malaccense*).

t. Santol (Sandoricum koetjape).—This is a medium sized tree, about 30 feet high, and bears round, yellowish fruits about 2 to 5 inches in diameter. It grows both wild and culti-vated and is often rather common. The fruits are covered with very short hairs and contain from two to five fairly large seeds, surrounded by a dirty white, soft, juicy, sour-sweet, edible pulp. The seeds are not eaten, only the sur-

FIGURE 79.—Rose apple (*Syzygium jambos*).

rounding pulp. Local names: *Sántol, sántu, séntol, sótol, sétol, kechápi, ketchápi, satúlu, wasúu, póno, kasápi, hasípi, keétol, sétung, séntul.*

97

u. Polynesian plum (Spondias dulcis).—This tree, 25 to 30 feet high, is widely distributed in Polynesia. It is often planted. The fruits are plumlike and are yellowish or yel-

FIGURE 80.—Santol (*Sandoricum koetjape*).

lowish-green. The thin pulp surrounding the large seed-bearing part is excellent to eat. While this species occurs also in some parts of Malaysia as a cultivated tree, its place in the forests is taken by a very similar species, *Spondias pinnata,* the fruits of which are also edible. Local names of *Spondias dulcis: Vi, wi, ivi, névie, vi-vao.* Of Spondias *pinnata: Kadóngdong, liwas, óntijo, ótjo, ulite, urital, váte, tetimur, nássou, ngólo, alubihon, libas, ádnas.*

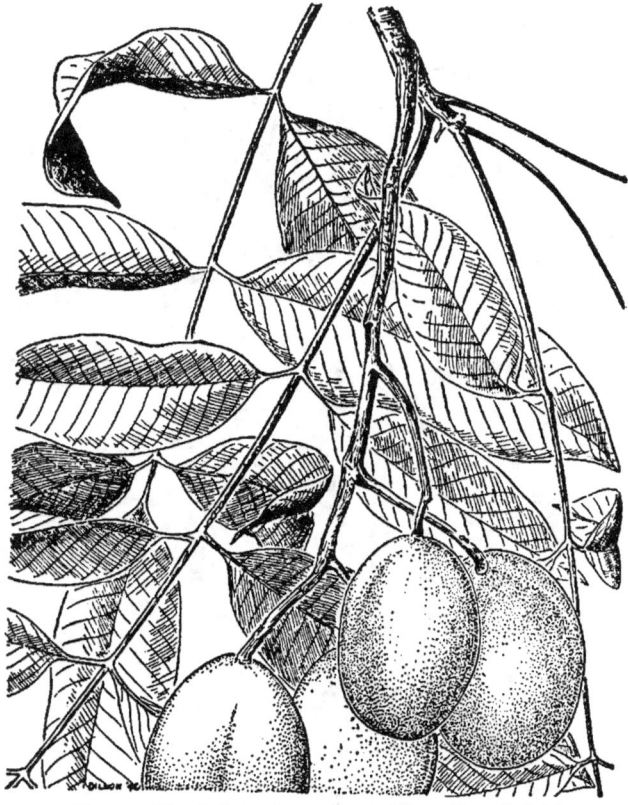

FIGURE 81.—Polynesian plum (*Spondias dulcis*).

v. Bilimbi and carambola.—These are small trees, 12 to 15 feet high, with green or pale green, very acid fruits which may be eaten raw or cooked. In one, the smooth fruits, similar to small green cucumbers, are borne on the trunks

99

and larger branches; in the other, the fruits borne on the small branchlets are sharply five-angled and star-shaped in cross section. Cultivated and wild in the settled areas, not

FIGURE 82.—Bilimbi and Carambola (A, *Averrhoa carambola*; B, *Averrhoa bilimbi*).

in the forests. Local names: *Balimbing, belimbing-mánis, belimbínes, balíbi, kámias, íba, urr-rúall, bull-rúall, arrafá-thna-owótrai, kalamías, kámias, garáhan-malibi, malimbin, tjalingting, limbi, libi, lumpias, lompiat, rumpiasa, pulirang, báknil, tueléla, tapréra, utéke, takuéle, tofúo.*

   w. Tamarind (Tamarindus indica).—This is a large tree,

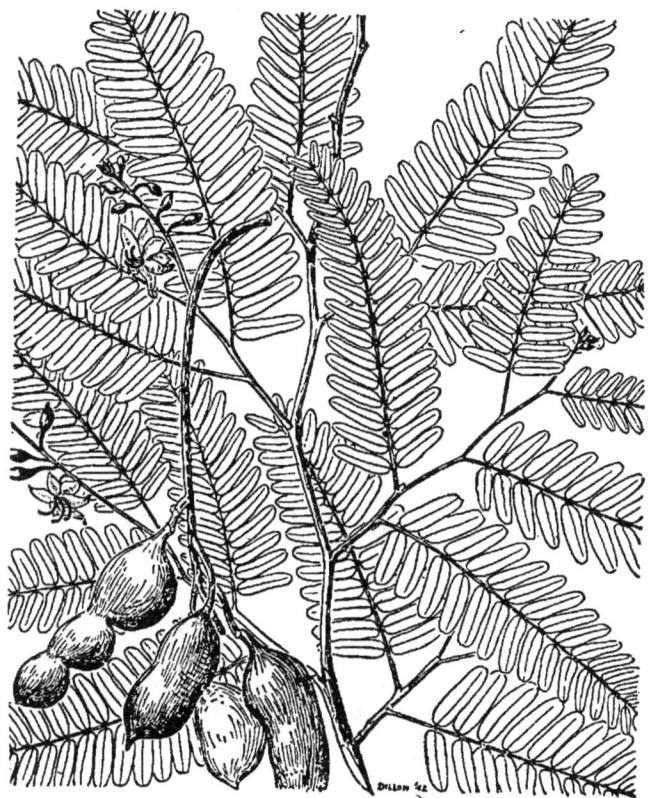

FIGURE 83.—Tamarind (*Tamarindus indica*).

often planted, sometimes wild, but not found in the forests. The fruit is brown. The acid pulp surrounding the seeds may be eaten; it is a mild laxative. The young leaves and flowers may be cooked and eaten as greens. Local names: *Ásam,*

ásam-djáwa, ásam-djow, átjem, káju-ásam, sampálok, átjam-tági, tamalági, tjumalági, tángkal-ásem, tjélagi, báge, kamáru, káza, helági, máke, máge, naáge, tóbi, sambálagi,

FIGURE 84.—*Cynometra cauliflora.*

tjámba, tjémpa, kenóbo, kiue, sukáer, au-máli, sáblaki, tobeláke.

x. *Cynometra cauliflora.*—This is a small tree, growing from 8 to 12 feet high. The flowers and fruits are borne on tuber-

cles on the trunk and larger branches.   The fruits are usually
ripe from August to November.   When ripe, the one-seeded
fruits are yellowish green or dirty yellow.   The parts sur-

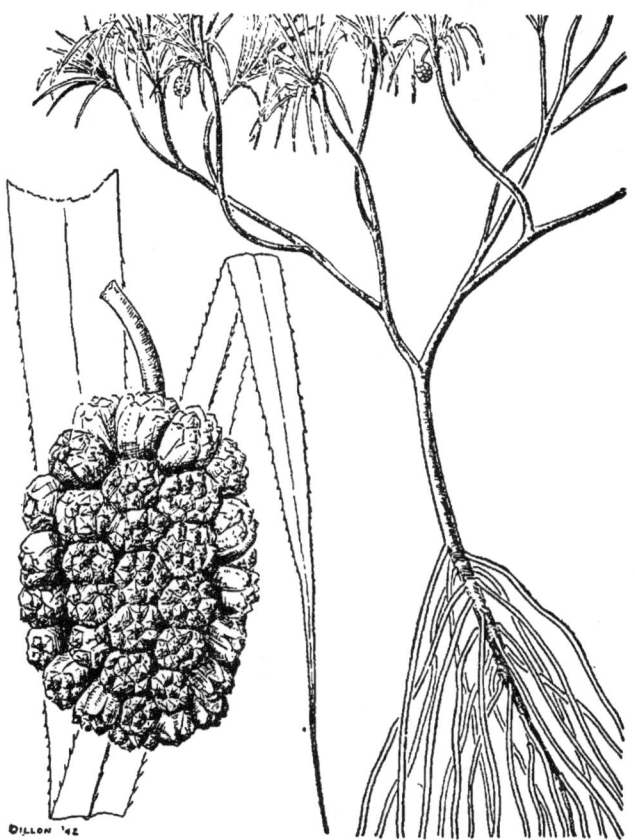

FIGURE 85.—Pandan or screw pine (*Pandanus tectorius*).

rounding the seed are yellowish white, fragrant, juicy, edible
and sweet-sour or sour in taste.   The tree does not occur
in the forests and is chiefly found only in cultivation.   Local
names: *nám-nam, námu-námu, nanámul, námet, añdjing-*

103

añdjing, lamúta, lamite, namúte, kéndis, alóma, kápi-ándjing, kuwándjo, pútji-ánggi, arípa, kanamále, klamúte.

y. Pandan or screw pine (Pandanus tectorius).—This is one of the most common plants in all of Polynesia and Malaysia, chiefly occurring near the sea and often forming dense thickets back of the beach. The trees are small, usually about 12 feet high. It may be identified by the prop roots on the trunk, or the long spiny leaves arranged spirally at the ends of the branches. The terminal tender leaf-bud or "cabbage" may be eaten raw or cooked. The scanty red fruit pulp is also edible, as are the small seeds. These statements apply to all of the numerous species of this genus in the forests of Malaysia, Micronesia, and Polynesia. Local names: *Fahola, ára, jahina, káju, hála, puliála, ággak, laujala, ietoga, pándan, pángdan, pondángo, póndak, pudako, paógo, óngor, baláwa, vádra, tóle, bónok, kéke-móni, háo-moni, káwae, órmon-jom, bánga, báku, bokúngo, hénak.*

z. Gnetum gnemon.—This is a small tree, 15 to 20 feet high, with glossy leaves and one-seeded red fruits. This is a forest tree, but it is sometimes planted. The seeds may be eaten raw, roasted, or boiled, and the young leaves make excellent greens. There are several other species; all, however, are woody vines and are found in the Malayan forests. Their seeds may also be eaten. Local names: *Bágo, bágu, banágo, bághu, nábo, ganému, súwah, blíndgo, wágu, súwa, húka, wa-sówa, uwáli, rúki, wáli.*

aa. Bignai (Antidesma bunius).—This is a small tree commonly found in open places and secondary forests. The numerous small, usually purplish-black, one-seeded fruits are edible. There are many other species of this genus in Malaya and a few in Polynesia, their fruits, all edible, are smaller than in bignai. Local names: *Bignai, búni, wúni, katakúti, kutikáta, búrneh, búne-tédong, húni.*

ab. Ximenia americana.—This is a small, spiny tree, always growing near the seashore. The rather scanty sour pulp surrounding the large hard seed-bearing part may be eaten raw, but the seeds should not be eaten. The young leaves also may be cooked and eaten. Local names: *Móli-tái, pi-od, sómi-sómi, túmi-túmi, paniúngan, bidára, bidára-laut, bidáro, wáma-wáma.*

ac. Wild tomato (Lycopersicum esculentum).—This wild form of the common cultivated tomato is an erect, branched

FIGURE 86.—*Gnetum gnemon.*

herb, 2 to 3 feet high, with leaves smaller than the cultivated form and small red fruit not larger than an English cherry. It is frequently common in deserted clearings, abandoned

105

agricultural lands, and at higher altitudes even in open grasslands. It does not occur in the forests. The small red fruits are eaten raw. Local names: *Kamátis, kamátis-búndok,*

FIGURE 87.—Bignai (*Antidesma bunius*).

kamántil, tamáte, tomáte, temántis, tómat, ránte, rántebéddhi, kendíri, kémir, ambélai, samáte, ántès, togálai, lambáte, matábai, kúet, kabótil, warasmála, samante.

ad. Ground cherry (Physalis (3 species)).—These may be identified as erect or ascending branched herbs with small white or yellow flowers. The round fruits are borne inside

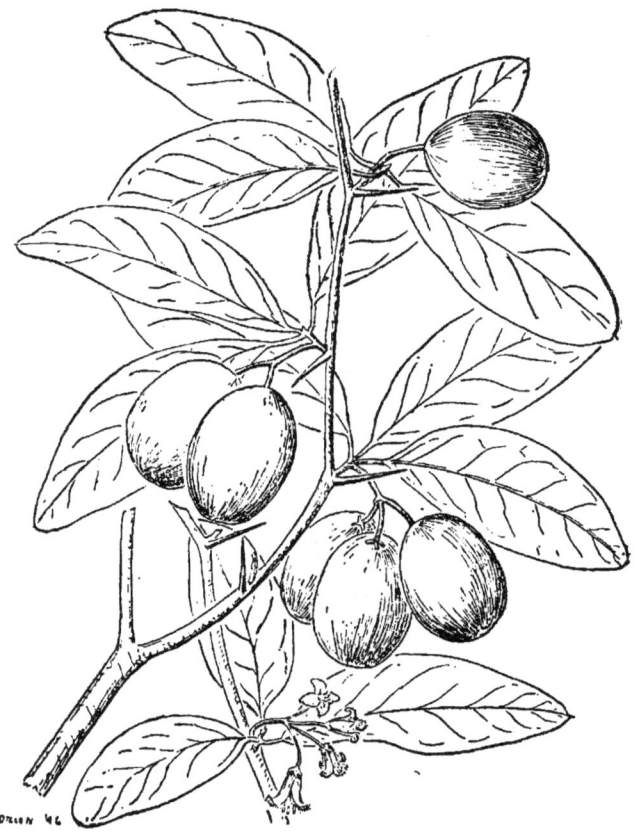

FIGURE 88.—*Ximenia americana.*

of an inflated husk. When mature, the fleshy round fruits are usually red. They somewhat resemble very small tomatoes and may be eaten raw. They are found in open waste

places, sometimes near the seashore, but not in the forests.
Local names: *Tomátes-kapúti, tomáte-cháka, tamánu-fairi,
póha, koníni, daun-bóba, daun-kópokópo, lelétop, tjetjéndit,*

FIGURE 89.—Wild tomato (*Lycopersicum esculentum*).

*tjeplúkan, jorjóran, kétjeplókan, dedédes, kenampok, kópok-
kopókan, léletóken, pádang-ráse, lápunónat, dágaméme,
putókun, sisiu, lápak-lápak.*

FIGURE 90.—Ground cherry (*Physalis* (3 species)).

SECTION XII

EDIBLE SEEDS

Paragraph

Plants whose seeds may be eaten_____ 23

FIGURE 91.—Pangi (*Pangium edule*).

■ 23. PLANTS WHOSE SEEDS MAY BE EATEN.—*a. Pangi (Pangium edule).*—This is a tree that grows 70 or 80 feet high.

It is found in humid forests and also often planted. The large fruits ((A), fig. 91) are up to 10 inches long, brown and densely rusty-hairy outside. The scanty pulp surrounding the numerous large hard seeds may be eaten when fully ripe. *Warning: The seeds (B) are very poisonous (hydrocyanic acid!). They are used as food by the natives but only after careful preparation. The seeds should be crushed and boiled for at least an hour, then put into running water for at least a day, after which they are boiled again and eaten; seek the assistance of competent natives if possible. The leaves also are poisonous if eaten.* Local names: *Pángi, pútjong, peétjong, pákem, kepájang, kukétong, kalówa, ngáfu.*

b. *Polynesian chestnut (Inocarpus fagiferus).*—This is a small or medium-sized tree, 8 to 10 or 20 feet high, much more common in Polynesia than in Malaysia. It grows especially near the seashore. The leaves are simple. The pods contain a single large seed which is an excellent food, when boiled or roasted, even better than the chestnut. Local names: *Íft, ifiméa, íhi, ívi, óle-ífi, íi, hi, híhi, gágan, gájam, áen, óno, aáne, aiáne, bosúa, bócu, buoy, bui, bénjek, gátet, gátep, gáe, gému, ankáeng, akádjeng, gáma, nías, eiáne, eiáno, kéam, kaéne, laiáno, ainhúal, mélc, mápe, ráta, rátti, émmer, gajámu, hájam, gugúra, gurámá, fuámoa, maráre, maárah, márrah, márau, maúpe, anillo, kuréak.*

c. *Sterculia foetida.*—This is a large tree with large red fruits. The numerous, nearly black seeds are rich in oil, the flavor somewhat suggesting the beechnut. The seeds may be eaten raw or roasted. Many other species of this genus occur in the forests but in most of them the leaves are simple. The seeds of all species are edible. Local names: *Kalúmpang, kajúmpang, kolómpang, halúmpang, kepóli, képah, kapáka, képuh, kalúpa, koleánga, poh, ghalómpang, kekepáhang, wúka, wúkak, bungóro, alúmpang, níta, nítas, fóngol, kailúpafúru.*

d. Indian almond (Terminalia catappa).—This is a large tree, generally found along the seashore but sometimes planted inland. Not uncommonly planted as a shade tree.

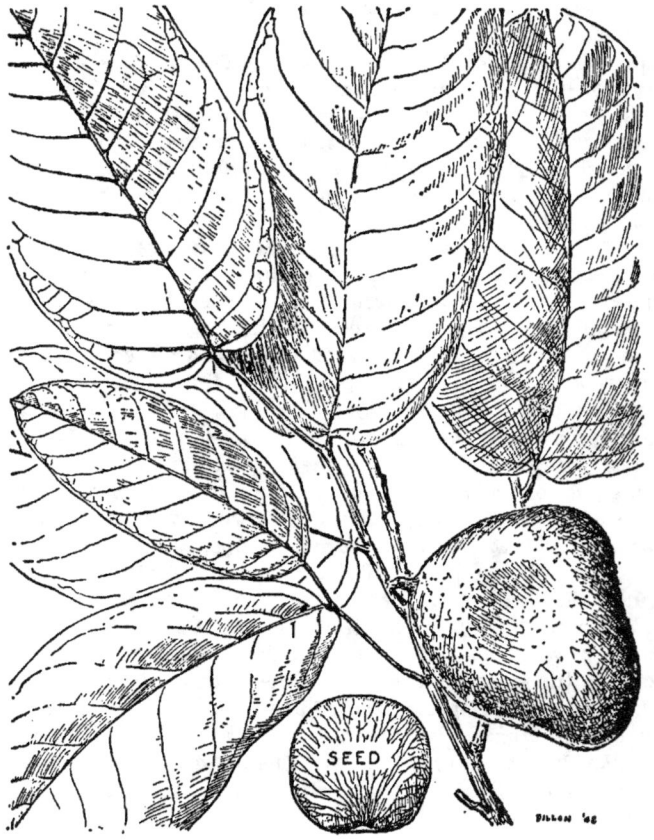

FIGURE 92.—Polynesian chestnut (*Inocarpus fagiferus*).

Some of the leaves are usually red. The fruits contain a single fair-sized seed which is of excellent flavor and may be eaten in any quantity.   Many other species of *Terminalia* occur in the forests, and the seeds of all are edible.   Local names: *Katápang, kaorika, kauarika, áua, autaráa, aásu,*

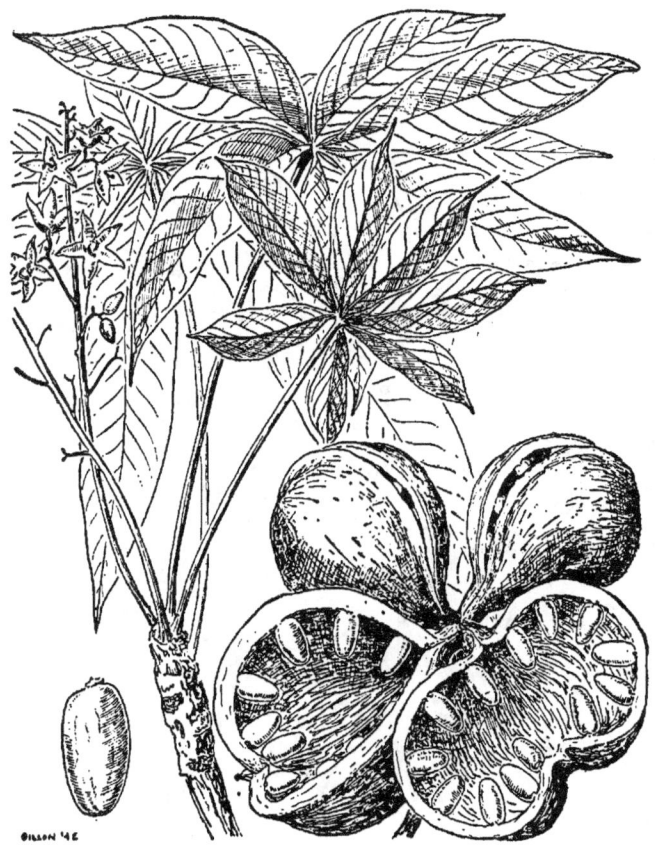

FIGURE 93.—Sterculia foetida.

asásu, auwiri, dáyle, ker, gúdill, sarf, tálie, tálie-úla, talisay, talése, tarísei, tási, talího, tavóla, ká, keime, ketápang, hatápang, atápang, lahápang, faoágia, ketápas, salrise, kamáni, lisa, wew, wéwa, sarísa, saliha, kális, kris, kauaríka, rúge, ngúsu, kell, sadína.

FIGURE 94.—Indian almond (*Terminalia catappa*).

e. Candle nut (Aleurites moluccana).—This is a common tree which may be identified by the foliage which is often pale green in contrast to that of other trees, or by the small

114

greenish white flowers. The fruits contain a single, hard-shelled seed rich in oil, and which may be eaten *after roasting*. Local names: *Kamíri, kemíri, kembíri, lúmbang, kukúi,*

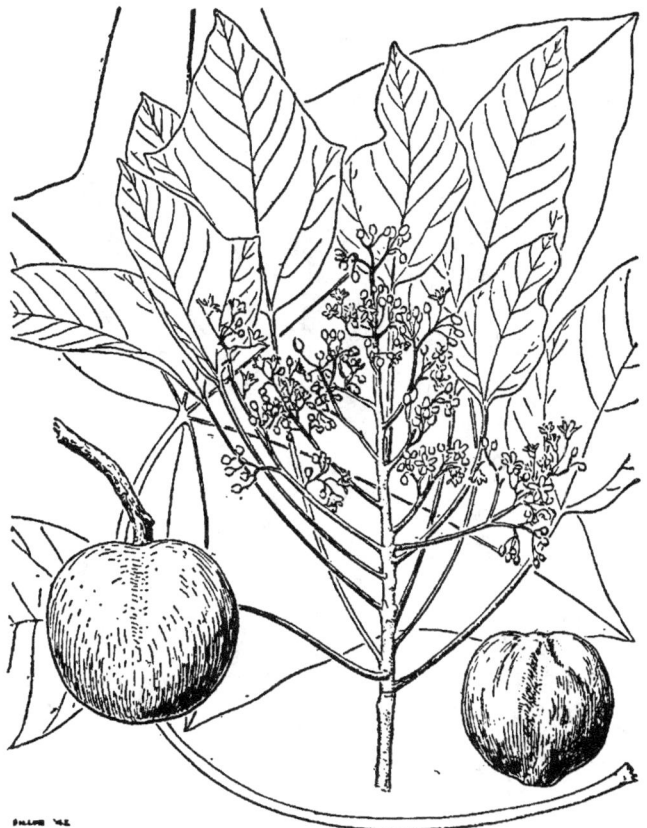

FIGURE 95.—Candle nut (*Aleurites moluccana*).

láma, keminting, muntjang, derékan, pidékan mére mírie, akmíri, imíle, umiri, lékong, kaléli, kawílu, kamie, kamíli, bajúe, lána, biúe, lepáti, lepóde, sapíri, ampíri, péleng, jéno, mílu, igúe, háge, háget, sakéta, hakáta, pojúem, húta, inhatch, láma, tia-íri, tutúi, tuitúi, nápa, váte, sikéci.

f. Cycas circinalis.—This is a palm-like plant with a rather rough stem and very stiff leaves, sometimes found in the for-

FIGURE 96.—*Cycas circinalis.*

est, more often near the seashore. The very young leaves ((B), fig. 96) which are seasonal, may be eaten cooked as asparagus. The trunk yields a kind of sago but its extraction is difficult. *Warning: The large seeds are used as food in times of scarcity but they are very poisonous unless properly prepared.* The flesh is crushed or grated and

FIGURE 97.—Kanari and pili (A, *Canarium commune;* B, *fruit of C. ovatum*).

soaked in water, with frequent changes of water, it being reported that this process should cover several days. The soaked material may be made into cakes and baked. *When-*

117

*ever possible, consult informed natives if the seed is to be
used as food.* Local names: *Báyit, bitógo, pitógo, pákisádji,
úta-niel, fádang, róro, nó-mall, brótel, frátel, rumiyan,
róro, fallútier, kokéal.*

g. *Kanari and pili (Canarium commune).—*There are many
kinds of *Canarium* in Malaya, the genus extending eastward
to Fiji and Samoa. They occur in the forests and are mostly
of large size. The sticky resinous sap of the bark is distinctly fragrant or aromatic. The very hard inner parts
of the fruit are usually more or less triangular in cross section, often pointed at the ends. The single, often fairly
large, oily seed is well-flavored, and may be eaten raw or
roasted. Some of the local names are: *Kanári, kánai, kanáli,
kiéri, nañari, nánai, pili, piláui, ifále, ihále, ifále, ifáne, inyat,
mafóa, núngi, ma-áli, aa-matie, mashóes, léhi, ihai, úpoi,
kódja, hihi, dédi, úwar, dokáe, hijáo, jálo, sében, ngie, niha,
njánja, njiára, njiha, hápo, hájo, sádjeng, ai-wikan.*

h. *Lotus (N e l u m b i u m n e l u m b o) and water lily
(Nymphaea).—*These plants both occur only in shallow fresh-
water lakes and in slow streams. The lotus flowers are pink
and the water lily flowers vary from white to pink or pale
blue. The large seeds of the lotus ((A), fig. 98) are excellent
when boiled or roasted, while the large roots, found in the
mud, may be cooked and eaten. Local names: *Báino, teráte,
taráte, sána, serodja.* The numerous small seeds of the water
lilies (B) may be cooked and eaten, as well as the more or
less thickened roots. Local names: *Lábas, laúas, púlau,
túndjung.*

i. *Pigeon pea (Cajanus cajan).—*This is a small shrub or
shrublike plant, 5 or 6 feet high, which is sometimes cultivated, but more often wild and frequently rather abundant.
It occurs in open places, never in the forests. The flowers are
yellow. The beans are edible but must be thoroughly cooked.
Local names: *Kádios, lébu, kátjang-káju, kátjang-iris,
kekátje, úndis, lebúi, legúi, tóri, sarupápa, bintótung, kántje,
túlis, túnis, túris, fúwe-jái, fúo-hóte.*

j. *Asparagus bean (Psophocarpus tetragonolobus).—*This is
a twining vine from somewhat tuberous roots, the flowers are
fairly large, and light violet-blue in color. The pods are 6 to

10 inches long, with four rather thin longitudinal wings. This is chiefly planted, but is sometimes found in fence rows. The tender pods, cooked as one would string beans, are an

FIGURE 98.—(A, Lotus (*Nelumbium nelumbo*); B, Water lily (*Nymphaea*).

excellent vegetable. The mature seeds may be roasted and eaten. Local names: *Ketjépir, tjipir, djáat, biráro, sárisre, kelóngkang, kalamismis, kamalúson, siguidíllas.*

119

k. Hyacinth bean (Dolichos lablab).—This vine bears violet or white flowers. The young pods are often somewhat pink or reddish. The seeds are white, yellowish with black

FIGURE 99.—Pigeon pea *(Cajanus cajan).*

dots, or black with white dots. It is often cultivated, and frequently found wild in thickets. The young pods, an excellent vegetable, may be cooked and eaten as one would string beans, and even the flowers and young leaves may be cooked and eaten, as well as the ripe seeds. Local names:

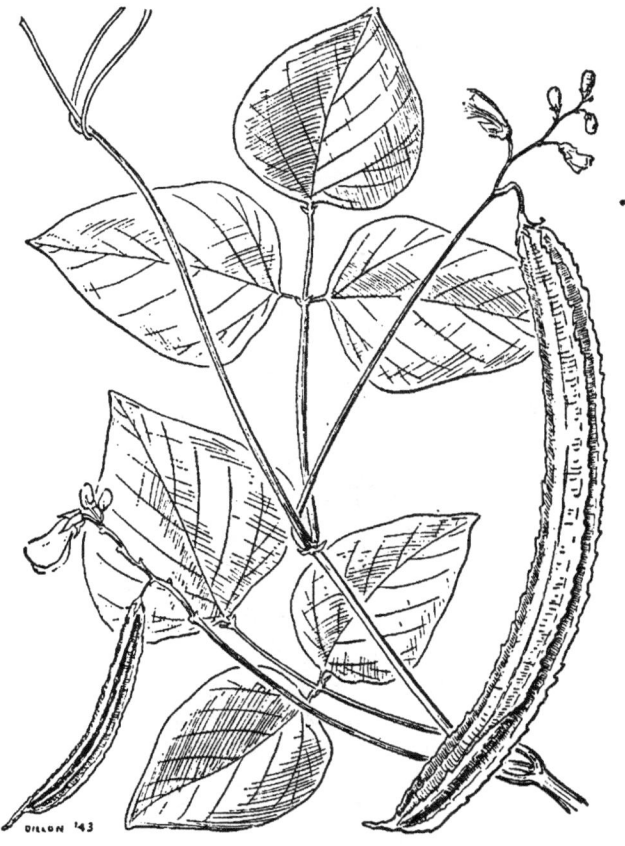

FIGURE 100.—Asparagus bean (*Psophocarpus tetragonolobus*).

Kára, kára-kára, kátjang-bádo, kátjang-péda, kekára, raoj-bédog, roaj-péda, koómas, kómak, rakára, bátau, búlai, sibáchi, arbíla, ndóto, lóto, papápa, chuchuméco, róto.

l. Lima bean (Phaseolus lunatus).—This vine has small flowers, greenish, sometimes white or violet within. It is cultivated and naturalized, the wild form occurring in

FIGURE 101.—Hyacinth bean (*Dolichos lablab*).

thickets. The very young tender pods may be cooked and eaten as one would prepare string beans. *Warning: The mature seeds are often very poisonous (hydrocyanic acid!)*, *and one must be very careful when dealing with the wild forms, especially those with black seeds.* The seeds vary in size and in color, ranging from white to brown or mottled or

FIGURE 102.—Lima bean (*Phaseolus lunatus*).

even jet black. The mature seeds of these wild forms may be eaten only after greatly prolonged cooking with many changes of water. Local names: *Patáni, kekára, kára,*

516614°—43——9   123

krátok, karátok, bédar, kéddar, krópook, róaj, róaj-cápri, róaj-hédjo, róak-gáling, buringi, butingi.

   m. Peanut (Arachis hypogaea).—The common peanut is

FIGURE 103.—Peanut (*Arachis hypogaea*).

often planted, especially in sandy soils. The fruits, borne under the surface of the ground, are very nutritious and the seeds may be eaten raw or cooked. Local names: *Mani,*

*kátjang-bróel, kátjang-táno, kátjang-támo, kátjang-tjina,
kátjang-djána, kátjang-maníla, kátjang-góreng, kakahúati,
hánsang, alítak, arítak, kásang, kása-góre, rétak-tánah,
rétak-gúring, ítak-búmi, bótji, baútji, boútji, njiha-tjína,
waráge, warápe, wehrápe, hatilal-únsil, hói, huwéa, hatila-
laitáin, uwársin, jongári-tjína, laúrur-makaharére, bóee,
joée-káse, jóre-rái, tjangóre, sanggóren, tjanggóreng.*

SECTION XIII

POISONOUS PLANTS

■ **24. PLANTS TO AVOID.—*a. Physic nut (Jatropha curcas).*—**
This is a very common shrub found in hedges and fence
rows. *Warning: The rather large seeds are poisonous and
violently purgative, not to be eaten under any circumstances.*
Local names: *Djárak-kósta, lau-páta, túba-túba, bindálo,
bintálo, úto-papalági, balátjai, dámar-énde, djirak, kaléke,
béaw, biue, péleng-kalíki, pákie-káse, moúen-máv, malóte,
mákamále, ai-kamáne, jáihua-kamálo, balátjai, bolátjai,
kadóto.*

b. Castor oil plant (Ricinus communis).—This is a common, coarse, erect shrub or shrublike plant with large lobed
leaves. It is found in thickets and open places. *Warning:
The seeds are poisonous and a violent purgative, not to be
eaten under any circumstances.* Local names: *Agaliya, djá-
rak, tángan-tángan, lúlang, dúlang, lajándru, rángam, kaliki,
tatánga, lólo, ketówang, kolónjan, alále, kilále, tilalóngi, lúlu,
lúluk, balátjai, tuitui-pakarángi.*

c. Tree nettle (Laportea).—These shrubs, or small trees,
grow in secondary forests and thickets, some species in the
high forest. There are many species. The leaf-edges, nerves,
leaf-stalks, flower- and fruit-bearing parts are supplied with
stiff, very sharp, stinging hairs, often not conspicuous. These
stinging hairs ((A), fig. 106) seated on thin bulbs, are filled
with intensely irritating sap. On light contact with the skin
one immediately has the sensation of having touched a very

hot iron, due, apparently, to the formic acid in the hair-sap. While intensely painful, the sting is normally not dangerous. Local names: *Ságai, sági, langáton; lingáton, anúling, lípa,*

FIGURE 104.—Physic nut (*Jatropha curcas*).

lípai, lúpa, daun-gátee, sála, sosóro-bátja, kemáduh, kemáduh-kébo, sóro-bilalágo, sosóro-bobúdo, láteng, keláting, púlus, saláto, lelésc, élat, karktáo, káhtat, káhtl, lilíes.

126

d. Tree nettle (Laportea).—This plant is one of the forms with larger, broader leaves from the southwestern Pacific area. The stinging properties and local names are the same

DILLON '42

FIGURE 105.—Castor oil plant (*Ricinus communis*).

as for the narrower-leafed form (*c* above). The numerous small flowers are greenish or greenish white in all these tree nettles. Figure 107 (A) shows a stinging hair enlarged. The curious thing about these tree nettles is that if one grasps

127

the leaves very firmly the result is usually little or no stinging, the stinging hairs being crushed. A light touch, however, usually results in an immediate burning sensation. Some species are much more irritating than others.

FIGURE 106.—Tree nettle (*Laportea*).

e. Cowhage (*Mucuna pruriens; M. biplicata; M. cyanosperma*).—These vines occur in thickets and secondary forests, usually not in the high forest. The flowers are greenish-

128

white to very dark purple or even red. A number of different species occur in Malaya, some without stinging hairs. Parts of the flowers and the pods are covered with many stiff, easily

FIGURE 107.—Tree nettle (*Laportea*).

detached, stinging hairs ((C), fig. 108 much enlarged). While distinctly irritating, they are not poisonous, being mechanical irritants. One should avoid getting these stinging hairs into the eyes, as then they cause intense inflammation and may be really dangerous. Local names: *Gónseng, kekára-gátel, keráwe, kárung, rarawéje, kówas, ípe, líkai, nipai, lúpoi, alilipai, danipai, dúglo, bukitkit.*

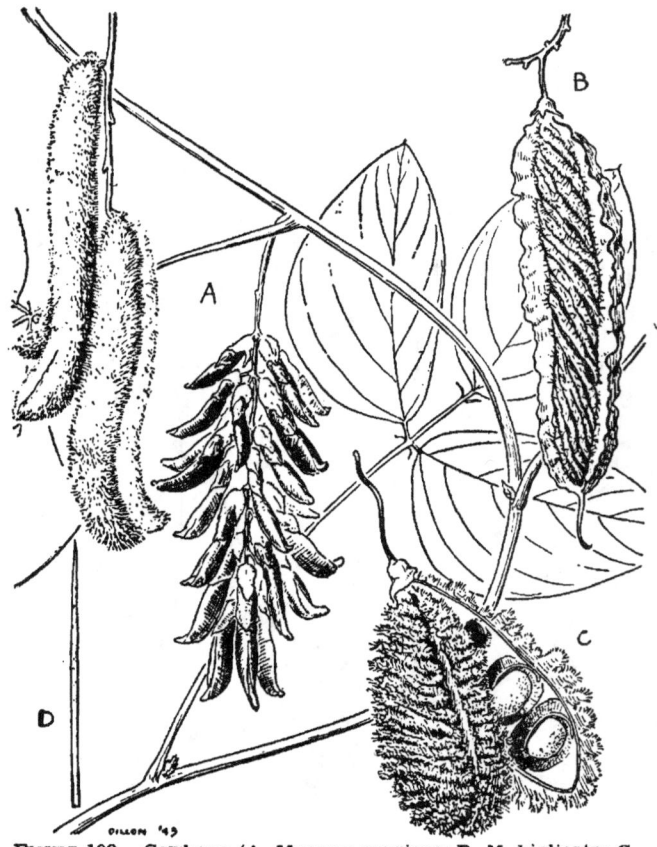

FIGURE 108.—Cowhage (A, *Mucuna pruriens;* B, *M. biplicata;* C, *M. cyanosperma*).

f. Semecarpus.—These shrubs, or small trees, sometimes grow to a height of 30 feet and chiefly occur in thickets and in the secondary forests, many different kinds being known. *Some of the species are reputed to cause bad skin eruptions on contact, or from the sap if the trees are cut down.* The fleshy

FIGURE 109.—*Semecarpus.*

swollen basal parts of the fruits are usually dark purple and can be eaten with safety. The plant belongs in the same family with poison ivy and poison oak. Treatment, if one is

131

poisoned, is the same as that indicated for poison ivy infections. These plants are not very dangerous. Local names: *Rángas, réngaspúteh, káju-sáju, léwer, lénat, rénat laulási, ingas, télik, ágas, anágas, hanágas, libas, ligas, lángas, párau, pánau, tóhnget, tóngot, tschóngot.*

Section XIV

PLANTS USED TO STUPEFY FISH

■ 25. PLANTS IN GENERAL.—*a.* In many parts of the region covered by this manual portions of several different kinds of plants are used to stupefy fish, both those found in tide pools and in small streams. The methods vary, but the usual one is to pound or crush the plant parts used, mix with water, and throw a sufficiently large quantity of the material into pools which the fish inhabit. In streams the material is always placed at the upper end of a quiet pool, thus permitting the current to spread it. Usually large quantities of this mixture must be used. The fish are suffocated, and usually come to the surface belly up; they can then be taken easily. The materials used for this purpose in no manner affect the flesh, and fish thus secured can be eaten with entire safety. *Whenever possible seek the advice of friendly natives as to what plants and what plant parts may be used for this purpose and how they are used.*

b. The most commonly used and most commonly available plants are different types of *Derris* (par. 26*b*), all woody vines, widely known as *tuba,* and also as *tugli, tubli, kaju tuba, toba, mombul, manengop, yup, duup, duva* and *nathon.* The fish poison is most abundant in the roots, but in preparing the material both the roots and other parts of the plants are pounded and thrown into the water. *Derris* is the most efficient of the various plants used. The large one-seeded fruits of *Barringtonia asiatica* (par. 26*d*) are also used. This is a large tree with large, very smooth leaves, pink flowers, and one-seeded fruits that are square in cross-section. Its natural habitat is only along the seashore of Malaysia and parts of Polynesia. It is known as *putat laut, bitung, butun, hutun, keben, modgin, puutin, kun, futu, hutu, puting, utu, vutu, vup.* The large solitary seed is mashed and thrown into the pools where the fish occur. Another often used plant that is frequently fairly common, is the shrub or small tree *Croton tiglium* (par. 26a). The small seeds are crushed and used as in *Barringtonia*. The species is rather commonly found about settlements, near houses, and is naturalized in waste places; it does not occur in the forests. Some of the local names are *túba-túba, chemékian, cheráken, simalákian, pancháhar, adaládal, simúli, kówe, kamaisa, kamágsa, túba, makaisa. Tephrosia purpurea* (par. 26c) is a small shrub or somewhat woody herb with small purple flowers and a small flat pod. It is probably the most used fish poison in Polynesia and Micronesia, where it is widely distributed. The whole plant is pounded or crushed and thrown into the water. Local names: *Avása, hóra, hóla, ouhóla, kohúhu.* The word *tuba* which is widely used in Malaya and applied to a number of totally different plants usually indicates a plant that may be used for stupefying fish. Incidentally, a charge of dynamite or even a hand grenade thrown in a pool is a very effective way of stunning fish.

■ 26. SPECIFIC PLANTS.—*a. Croton oil plant (Croton tiglium).*—This shrub, or small tree, is cultivated and spontaneous. The seeds are used chiefly for poisoning fish. *Warning: A very violent purgative. Not to be eaten under any circumstances.* Local names: *Kamaisa, kamágsa, kemáde, makaisa, túba, tjerákin, similákian, kemalákijan, ádal-ádal, pentjáhar, rúngkou, dúngkow, lúngkow, lánta, kelmúre, túpo, humulite, semúli, kówe.*

b. *Derris elliptica.*—This is a most efficient fish poison, its use for suffocating fish in slow streams, pools, and even tide pools is widely known. There are many different species of the genus, some more potent than others. The parts used are chiefly the crushed roots, but sometimes the crushed

branches and leaves are also used. These are all woody vines,
with flowers resembling those of the bean, and narrowly

FIGURE 110.—Croton oil plant (*Croton tiglium*).

winged pods, occurring chiefly in thickets and secondary
forests. See paragraph 25 for methods of use and local
names.

134

c. Tephrosia purpurea.—This is a small, branched shrub or shrubby herb, growing in open places. The small flowers

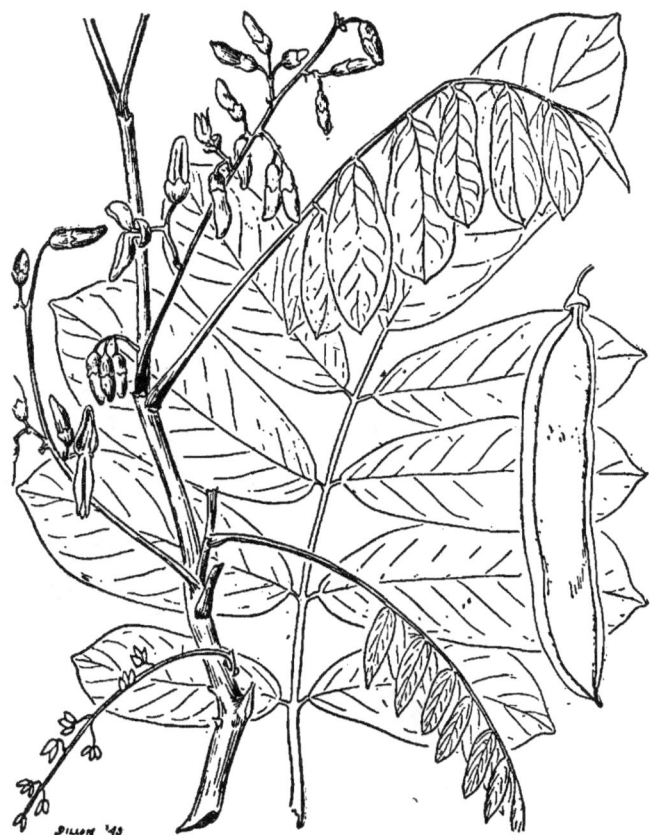

FIGURE 111.—*Derris elliptica.*

are purple. It is widely used as a fish poison, especially in Polynesia. The whole plant is crushed and thrown into the pools where fish occur. See paragraph 25 for local names.

135

d. Barringtonia asiatica.—These large trees grow on the seashore. They bear large smooth leaves, large pink flowers with many stamens, and large fruits which are square in cross

FIGURE 112.—*Tephrosia purpurea.*

section and which contain a single large seed. The crushed seeds are used for killing fish in pools. See paragraph 25 for local names and methods of use.

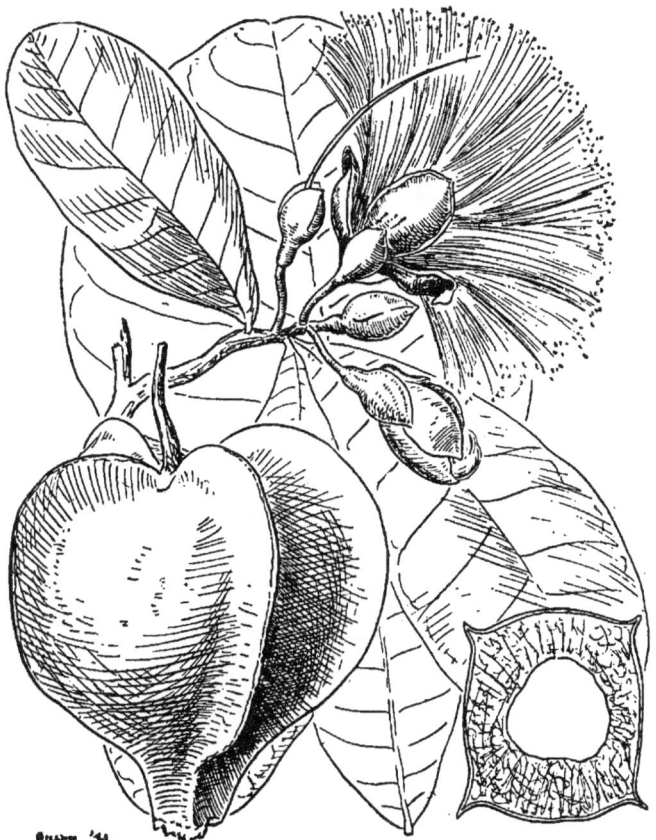

FIGURE 113.—*Barringtonia asiatica.*

INDEX

INDEX

○

Notes

Notes

Notes

Notes

Notes

Notes

<u>Notes</u>

www.ingramcontent.com/pod-product-compliance
Lightning Source LLC
Chambersburg PA
CBHW070354290526
45790CB00004B/1493